Along the Way

Real Life Moments Touched by God

Meredith® Books
Des Moines, Iowa

Meredith Books
1716 Locust Street
Des Moines, Iowa 50309-3023
meredithbooks.com
Printed in China
First Edition.
Library of Congress Control Number: 2007924916
ISBN 978-0-696-23398-2

Produced with the assistance of The Livingstone Corporation.
General editors: Betsy Schmitt, Linda Washington, Diane Stortz.
Project staff: Joel Bartlett, Larry Taylor, Kirk Luttrell, Linda Taylor.

Cover photograph copyright © Darrell Gulin/Stone/Getty Images

The following photography copyright iStockphoto®: Sas van Veen, 28; Robert Churchill, 38;
Francis Twitty, 63; Peter Galbraith, 75; Hunter Photography, 82; Edward Hardam, 90; Caroline
K. Smith, M.D., 101; Jason R. Warren, 136; Jeff Giniewicz, 144; Rave, 151; Dale Robbins, 166;
Dane Wirtzfeid, 194; Jan Rihak, 217; Larysa Dodz, 229. Shawn Taylor Photography, 109. Larry
P. Taylor, ltdltd, 113,125.

Scripture quotations marked AMP are from *The Amplified Bible*, Copyright © 1954, 1958, 1962,
1964, 1965, 1987 by The Lockman Foundation. All rights reserved. Used by permission.

Scripture quotations marked ESV are from the *Holy Bible, English Standard Version*, Copyright
© 2001 by Crossway Bibles, Good News Publishers. Used by permission. All rights reserved.

Scripture quotations marked NIV are from the *Holy Bible, New International Version*®. NIV®.
Copyright © 1973, 1978, 1984 International Bible Society. Used by permission. All rights
reserved.

Scripture quotations marked NKJV are from the *Holy Bible, New King James Version*, Copyright
© 1982 by Thomas Nelson, Inc. Used by permission. All rights reserved.

Scripture quotations marked NLT are from the *Holy Bible, New Living Translation*, Copyright
© 1996. Used by permission of Tyndale House Publishers, Inc., Wheaton, Illinois 60189. All
rights reserved.

Scripture quotations marked PHI are from *The New Testament in Modern English* by J. B. Phillips.
Copyright © by J. B. Phillips 1958, 1960, 1972. All rights reserved.

Scripture quotations marked TLB are taken from *The Living Bible,* Copyright ©1971. Used by
permission of Tyndale House Publishers, Inc., Wheaton, Illinois 60189. All rights reserved.

TABLE OF CONTENTS

Introduction 5

1 Nothing Is Impossible - *Discovering God's Limitless Power* 7
2 High Anxiety - *Leaping Out in Faith* 12
3 Concert of Praise - *Finding God in Barren Times* 15
4 Two Daughters—One Father - *Finding a Place in God's Family* 18
5 The Blind Shall See - *Seeing Jesus When Life Goes Dark* 23
6 At the Table of the King - *Finding Christmas in an Unexpected Place* . . .27
7 A Boy for Brutus - *Trusting God to Meet Our Needs* 31
8 Backpacker in the Rain - *Extending Acts of Mercy to Others* 36
9 A Mother's Day Flower - *Finding Worth in God's Eyes* 40
10 Raising Ashley - *Praying Through Life's Challenges* 43
11 Whom Do You Trust? - *Discovering God's Perfect Plan* 48
12 The Worry Stone - *Finding God's Answer to Worry* 52
13 Star Struck - *Finding God's Truth in Unlikely Places* 56
14 Beautiful Butterfly - *Learning About God's Compassion* 59
15 The Path to Restoration - *Working Through the Pain* 62
16 The Innkeeper - *Finding Goodness When You Least Expect It* 66
17 A Rebellious Sheep - *Following the Shepherd* 70
18 Practice Doesn't Make Perfect - *Finding Perfection in Jesus* 74
19 Freed to Forgive - *Finding Real Healing in Forgiveness* 78
20 "What's Your Friend's Name?" - *Knowing the Power of Jesus' Name* 81
21 Something Changed - *Experiencing the Power of God's Transforming Love* . .85
22 Jailhouse Faith - *Seeking God Wherever We Are* 89
23 No Agenda - *Influencing Others With Christ's Love* 93
24 The Sleep of the Innocent - *Resting in the Father's Constant Care* 97
25 Dismissed! - *Finding Forgiveness in an Unexpected Place* 100
26 Lost and Found - *Putting a Face to God's Loving Care* 105
27 I Surrender - *Acknowledging God's Place in Our Lives* 108
28 The Unexpected Gift - *Living in God's Love* 112
29 Uncharted Territory - *Navigating Life's Unexpected Turns* 116
30 Courtroom Drama - *Hearing From God Through His Word* 120

31 Huge and Scary - *Remembering How Big God Is* 124
32 Uprooted - *Finding God's Peace in Change* 128
33 Underwater Rescue - *Giving Credit to the Real Superhero* 131
34 The Least, the Lost, and the Lonely
       Discovering Jesus in a Garbage Dump 135
35 The Power of Love - *Dismantling the Walls Around People's Hearts* . . . 139
36 My Father's Taillights - *Following as God Leads* 143
37 A Song in the Dark - *Finding Courage to Face Our Fears* 147
38 Chance Meeting - *Receiving God's Unexpected Provision* 150
39 It's Not Fair - *Accepting Life's Disappointments* 154
40 The Art of Toilet Scrubbing - *Learning Humility in Menial Tasks* . . . 157
41 Crowds, Fish Oil, and Ego - *Letting God Take Us Where He Wants Us* . . 161
42 A Solid Foundation? - *Preserving a Good Foundation* 165
43 It Takes a Stable - *Facing Your Fears* 169
44 Class Reunion - *Seeing God Through Our Friendships* 174
45 Troubled Waters - *Experiencing Jesus in Life's Emergencies* 177
46 Free to Receive - *Understanding God's Faithfulness* 180
47 Transformed by Love - *Discovering the Power of God's Great Love* . . . 184
48 Standing Guard - *Discerning God's Protection* 188
49 One Way to America, Please -
       Learning to Wait as God Works Behind the Scenes 193
50 A Doubter's Prayer - *Meeting God Through Uncertainties* 198
51 The Writing on the Wall - *Remembering God's Constant Presence* . . . 202
52 A Special Girl - *Praying for God to Work in Someone's Life* 206
53 More Than Words Can Say - *Loving for the Long Haul* 209
54 Sleepless - *Resting in the Lord* 212
55 Blunder Down Under - *Understanding the Value of Friendships* 216
56 Fireflies - *Grasping the Truth of God's Persistence and Presence* 220
57 A Divine Embrace - *Finding God's Comfort in a Child's Hug* 224
58 Miss(ed) Hospitality - *Learning to Open Heart and Home* 228
59 The Little Mother - *Learning to Cope Through Life's Difficulties* 233
60 A Friend Few Can Claim - *Reaping the Power of Daily Prayer* 237
61 Turkey and Trouble - *Tapping Into God's Amazing Peace* 240
62 All Things New - *Finding New Beginnings in Brokenness* 243

Author Bios 247
Topical Index 250
Scripture Index 253

INTRODUCTION

Two people were walking on the road from Jerusalem to the village of Emmaus. As the Gospel of Luke records, it was the day after Resurrection Sunday, a day filled with rumors and uncertainty, sorrow and hope. A stranger joined the pair as they walked and talked. He seemed oddly unaware of the tumultuous events of the past few days: the arrival in Jerusalem of Jesus of Nazareth, whom many thought to be the Messiah; his arrest; his crucifixion. And now stories were swirling that his tomb was empty, that he had been seen by his disciples, that he was alive.

The three continued their discussion as they traveled until dusk, when they arrived in Emmaus. The two invited the stranger to stay with them for the night and as they sat at the dinner table, the stranger took some bread, broke it, and handed it to them. And they recognized him for who he was: Jesus. In an instant he disappeared. "Were not our hearts burning within us while he talked with us on the road and opened the Scriptures to us?" they asked one another.

The chapters of this book, we pray, will be to you like the Emmaus road experience of those two travelers. These true stories describe people walking through the everyday circumstances of life—some happy, some sad, some momentous, some minor. But in all of the stories, the writers realize that Jesus has indeed been there with them as they traveled along the way. And as a result their hearts have been warmed and their lives have been changed.

1 Nothing Is Impossible
Discovering God's Limitless Power

Jim Davidson was my father's best friend. They had the kind of friendship that turns men into mischievous boys when they're together. Whether playing tennis, horsing around in the swimming pool with their children, watching a ball game, or teasing their wives, they cherished their time together. But the year my dad was 42 years old, their friendship was severely tested.

One morning at 2 a.m. my father awoke screaming with a violent seizure that knocked him out of bed and onto the floor. I rushed into my mom and dad's bedroom.

"Help me keep him from biting his tongue or hurting himself!" Mom directed.

Dad's right side flailed and his screams evolved into moans as his jaws clamped shut. I held him—partly to protect him, partly to comfort myself—and prayed fervently for God to end the seizure. Finally it subsided.

Dad was exhausted, confused, and frightened. I was just glad he was still alive. We immediately called Jim Davidson to help us get him to the hospital.

We waited at the hospital until morning while doctors and nurses performed tests. We learned the cause of the massive seizure: My strong, athletic dad had a very aggressive malignant brain tumor. Even with surgery and chemotherapy the doctor said Dad had only six months to live.

In a few hours our family and our world turned upside down. We clung to one another and to Jesus.

Jim constantly encouraged Dad. He stood by him through the surgery, recovery, and trips to the hospital for chemo. In between these times he let Dad win at chess.

As the tumor took over more of Dad's brain, he suffered excruciating seizures and headaches. He became paralyzed on his right side, lost much of his vision, and began losing his ability to speak. Jim's faith and humor kept Dad's spirits up and hope alive.

When an insurance calamity left my family with more than $100,000 in unpaid medical bills, Jim had confidence that everything would work out. One crisp Saturday morning, Jim came by, as was his custom, and took Dad for a walk, pushing his wheelchair. Jim insisted that Mom and I join them. The four of us walked, talked, and prayed. Then, ignoring Dad's wishes, we went to the nearby golf clubhouse "to see who was out and about."

The club was strangely vacant. Jim asked me to hold open the back door of the building while he pushed Dad outside toward the first tee. As they passed through the door, the sun glistened on Dad's wheelchair, and cheers and applause erupted—more than 150 friends and neighbors filled the patio area! Jim took center stage to announce the start of Dad's benefit golf-a-thon.

The joy of that day was unbelievable. My father received an unending stream of hugs and encouragement. He was radiant. And although he had trouble staying alert for more than two hours at a time, he spent seven hours at the event with energy to spare and a smile that never waned. When the last hole of golf was played, Jim announced that more than enough had been raised for my dad's medical care. That day, Jesus wore Jim's skin.

The hospital trips increased. Despite all the treatments and medication, the tumor was growing back and spreading rapidly.

Then one Saturday morning in November, Jim did not come over as he had every weekend since Dad's tumor was discovered in August. He never again visited or called. Jim worked for a large company and had been transferred, and I learned that Jim and his family had quickly and quietly moved to another state. Jim had known for some time that his departure was coming, but he couldn't bring himself to say goodbye to his dying friend, so he left without a word.

Dad was devastated. At first he refused to believe that Jim was really gone. I took him to Jim's house to see the For Sale sign and to stare through the windows into the empty rooms. Dad had to accept the sad reality of Jim's absence.

The tumor had affected Dad's emotions. He cried, and sometimes wailed, for the return of his friend, Jim Davidson. He prayed with halting words, "Lord, I knowwww . . . youuu will . . . brrrring Jim Davidson back, in Jeeeesus' name." He found comfort in Luke 1:37: "For nothing is impossible with God" (NIV). He took this promise at face value and prayed repeatedly in Jesus' name that the Lord would bring Jim Davidson back.

He prayed with halting words, "Lord, I knowwww . . . youuu will . . . brrrring Jim Davidson back, in Jeeeesus' name."

I didn't want him to be hurt even more by misinterpreting Scripture. I felt I had to step in. "Dad, I don't think God exactly meant that we are to expect him to move heaven and earth to accommodate our personal requests. Jim Davidson made a bad decision, but he's not coming back. God won't bring him back, but he will help heal the hurt Jim caused you."

Dad kept praying and believing that God would bring Jim Davidson back to him.

Two weeks passed and Sunday came. We attended a large church with many services, and we decided to go to the evening service so Dad could rest in the morning. After the service we waited until nearly everyone had exited before navigating the wheelchair toward the door. A kind-looking man, whom I didn't recognize and who looked about 10 years older than my dad, approached and stood before us.

This man, with compassion and joy in his eyes, reached down to take Dad's paralyzed hand in his. He said, "I realize you don't know me, but I have seen you every week and have been praying for you. God has spoken to my heart. While I don't know what you're facing, I feel called to help you through it. If I can do anything, I am here for you. I want to be your friend." He closed his hands around Dad's hand and said, "My name is Jim Davidson."

Mom and I broke into tears. Dad also wept for joy, and in his halting speech, repeated praises to God. We finally explained what was going on to the startled Mr. Davidson. Then he too felt blessed by God's unmistakable fingerprint on the situation.

The new Jim Davidson strengthened my dad with his friendship until Dad died six weeks later. His final healing had come, and he was where he so longed to be—in Jesus' arms. By God's grace, never again will I limit what God can do. He can do the impossible.

—Tom Burggraf

WHEN GOD BREAKS THROUGH

Childlike faith should be the rule for Jesus' followers, not the exception. Jesus explained, "I tell you the truth, unless you change and become like little children, you will never enter the kingdom of heaven" (Matthew 18:3, NIV). We never need to convince ourselves that God is somehow not able or willing to do the impossible for us, his precious children, and we never need to convince anyone with childlike faith that Jesus will not do just what he said he would do. Childlike faith paves the way for the miraculous.

Are you facing an impossible situation right now? If not, you will someday soon. When you do, remember the word *impossible* is not in God's vocabulary. He will make a way in the wilderness for you. Trust in him as his child. It's not at all foolish; it's the only wise choice.

MY CHALLENGE

Do you need a miracle? Who among us doesn't? Ask him. Trust him. Rest in him. Just like a child. And then expect the impossible. Remember: "For nothing is impossible with God" (Luke 1:37, NIV).

2 HIGH ANXIETY
Leaping Out in Faith

"You can do it!" my friends called to me. However they weren't the ones standing on the tiny platform attached to a towering tree 50 feet off the ground!

"Just jump and grab the bar in front of you!" they encouraged.

Still I hesitated. "You're fine," said the teenage coach standing near me on a branch. "You've come this far. You can do this."

As a parent I'd been invited to experience this Young Life camp firsthand. Up to this point the ropes course had been challenging but fun. Now, however, as I realized I had to leap into the air to finish, my heart pounded in my ears and my stomach clenched. The safety rope attached to my waist didn't alleviate my fears.

"Let me go down another way!" I begged. After all I was 53 years old.

"There is no other way," the coach explained.

"What about a ladder—or a helicopter?" I wasn't joking.

Patiently my young coach explained the spiritual analogy of the jump. "It's like trusting Jesus," he said. "When we put our lives in the hands of the Savior, he's there for us no matter what. Trust me, when you take this leap of faith leaving your fears on this platform, you'll discover the power of trust. Fixing your eyes on Jesus and stepping out in faith is how to trust him no matter what comes into your life."

"Help me, Jesus," I whispered. I focused on the bar in front of me, breathed in hard, and leaped into the air. Cheers rose from the crowd below as my hands closed over the bar. My heart swelled with exhilaration as I was lowered to the ground.

Twenty years later God challenged me to take a mission trip to Kenya. By this time I had learned that whenever God called me to a new challenge, he already knew that I could not accomplish it by my own strength or abilities. Instead I would have to step out into the unknown, solely trusting Jesus to provide and guide me. So I began planning my trip.

But as the time to leave approached, I began to doubt. *Why am I doing this? Why should I leave my cozy life and go to a place where I know no one and have no idea what I will encounter? Malaria, typhoid, AIDS? Weird food? Unknown languages? Snakes?* I was a healthy woman for 73, but what if my body suddenly rebelled? What if I became ill so far from home?

It would be much safer and easier to stay in my comfort zone, to cling to my tree of security. But each time those thoughts flooded my heart and mind, God reaffirmed that I was to go and trust him.

So I went. Trusting him, I flew to Kenya. Trusting him, I worked with a Christian ministry that educates and provides homes for teenage orphans. Trusting him, I taught young women the Bible, English, music, sewing, and health so they would have skills to find jobs.

Why am I doing this? Why should I leave my cozy life and go to a place where I know no one . . .

As I trusted God to guide and help me be a leader, teacher, and friend to these young women, I discovered again that when he calls us to a task, he equips and empowers, blesses, and gives peace.

—*Barbara Collier*

WHEN GOD BREAKS THROUGH

Each challenge in life involves danger or discomfort. When God brings a new stage or experience into our lives, we can step out and face the unknown or we can hang back, but we only see God's work if we are willing to take a risk. As we face our changing circumstances, we can trust our unchanging God.

In the midst of national turmoil, the prophet Isaiah wrote, "You will keep in perfect peace all who trust in you, whose thoughts are fixed on you!" (Isaiah 26:3–4, NLT). God has promised that when we keep our eyes fixed on him, we will have peace, perfect peace that comes only from him. We can trust our Master with our very lives, no matter how high the tree.

MY CHALLENGE

What challenge do you face today? What is God prompting you to do that has paralyzed you with fear and doubt? Write a letter to God telling him exactly how you feel about meeting this challenge and what you fear. Ask him to give you the strength you need to take the risk. Ask God to help you discover the peace that comes from trusting him.

3 CONCERT OF PRAISE
Finding God in Barren Times

Escape. I needed to escape. I had to get away.

So for two hours I hiked aimlessly through freshly planted cornfields and the dry, brittle grasslands around my small Nebraska college. Finally I discovered a minuscule brook and sat on its bank. Perhaps no one even knew the brook was here. It was alone, like me.

I took off my hoodie so the spring sun could warm my winter-pasty skin. A soft breeze tickled the grasses.

How long have I lived here now? . . . Seven excruciating months, but it seems like forever. No movie theater, no mall, no Starbucks, not even a McDonald's.

At first I'd been thrilled at the opportunity to get an education and had hoped for a roommate who would become a good friend. But my assigned roommate didn't want to be in college and hated sharing a room. So I spent most of my time escaping from her and our room, even though I longed for my own space.

My parents didn't understand my situation. "Hang in there, dear. Just be more positive," they told me.

Well, I'd been positive, constructive, and creative. I found friends; I sang in the choir; I attended all the special events and games. I kept a journal and I even learned to knit. And, of course, I studied. But an 18-year-old raised in the city can only find so much to do in a cornfield-shrouded college. I had run out of creative juices mid-January. The winter hadn't brought enough snow to cross-country ski—one of my outlets for stress. But the temperatures had been bitterly cold—too cold to wander far from campus on foot. Freshmen weren't allowed to have cars, and I had no upperclassmen friends with cars, so I couldn't even get off campus for a quick diversion. College began to feel more like prison than a first taste of freedom. Now, at the end of March, I was suffocating in the smallness of my world.

I lay down in the tall, stiff grass and pondered the absence of clouds in the pale blue sky. Intense sunlight massaged my face. I closed my eyes and listened.

The brook continued to gurgle. I listened more intently.

As the breeze nudged the grasses, the sound of their movement became almost deafening. "Let everything that breathes sing praises to the Lord! Praise the Lord! The Lord is God! The Lord is God!" they seemed to cry.

Would I praise God along with the grasses and the stream? Would I praise him no matter what my circumstances?

It's a language—the language of nature! I realized. *A private celebration, a song of nature just for God—and I can hear it!*

After all Scripture said something about if people didn't praise God then nature would cry out. I felt a sudden challenge in my spirit. Would I praise God along with the grasses and the stream? Would I praise him no matter what my circumstances?

I closed my eyes and added my own song of praise: "Thank you, Lord. You are truly awesome in every way. Teach me to recognize your movement in my world and to praise you every day."

In that moment, I realized that I was miserable because my vision and hearing were so limited. I needed to start seeing the marvels in even the simplest things. A concert of praise had been going on all around me, but I had not been listening.

Refreshed and renewed, I stood up. Now, which way was the dorm?

—*Gloria Spielman*

When God Breaks Through

Whenever we feel alone or lost in a situation we can't control, we can still find reason to sing praise: "The Lord is God!" We may feel small and insignificant, like blades of grass or a tiny brook. But God sustains and nurtures even the smallest parts of creation. If he cares for the grasses, he will take care of us. When we are parched and lonely, God will breathe a song into us, and praise is the key.

My Challenge

Find a place where you can enjoy nature—a park, the beach, your own backyard. Concentrate on the sights and sounds and let them draw you closer to God. Let the psalmist's words direct your thoughts: "Shout with joy to the Lord, O earth! Worship the Lord with gladness. Come before him, singing with joy. Acknowledge that the Lord is God! He made us, and we are his" (Psalm 100:1–3, NLT).

Imagine that the sounds you hear—the trees rustled by the wind, the birds singing—are joining you in this praise chorus. Thank God for the way nature speaks to your senses and look and listen for what God says to you through his creation.

---

4 TWO DAUGHTERS— ONE FATHER

Finding a Place in God's Family

Spring often arrives late on Cape Cod, like a tourist who somewhere took a wrong turn. The year that both of our daughters turned 16, though, spring was right on time.

Patches of daffodils dotted the streets of our small village like broken shards of sun. Amber and Sarah loved these harbingers of spring and often posed for birthday photos surrounded by the splashes of yellow. This year, however, they were two young women on a mission. The joint birthday celebration we always held was over, their friends hastily sent on their way. I had begun to clean up the aftermath, but the girls would have none of it.

"It's time, Mom," Amber said impatiently.

"You promised you'd take us to get our permits today," Sarah added. "It's already 3:00 and the DMV closes at 5:00. Can't we hurry?"

How could I forget? The girls had talked of little else as "Sweet Sixteen" approached. Getting their driver's permits was the birthday gift they wanted most of all, and they were not about to let me forget it.

Amber and Sarah were not the only teenagers in our home eager for wheels and independence. Their older brother Adam and younger brothers Matt and Jordan were constantly on the go as well. Adam, Amber, and Jordan were born to us, but Sarah and Matt had come to us three years

LONG THE WAY

earlier when a crisis in their home left them with no custodial parent. Sarah and Amber became fast friends in fourth grade when they discovered their mutual birthday, and every year since the girls had celebrated together. The close friends had now become sisters—foster sisters.

And I was their mom. Qualifying adjectives like *foster, adoptive,* or *biological* don't matter when you're raising children. For the years that my husband and I were privileged to have Sarah and Matt, I was their mom. Period.

The teenage years are a challenge whether you have one teen or five at a time, as we did. Yet never once during their adolescent years did our biological kids even hint that we shouldn't have opened our home to two more children. They accepted their new siblings into our family as God accepts us—without qualification.

Despite the differences in how they had been raised, Amber and Sarah had much in common: the same birth date, school friends, and church youth group. One was first-chair clarinet in the school band, the other second-chair. Both were excellent students.

As the girls moved into their high school years, however, profound differences emerged. One liked jazz, the other rock. One wanted the best grades, the other the most friends. One dressed conservatively, the other trendier. Once close friends and allies, the girls now

Neither wanted to come in second in anything, and that included getting her driver's license.

seemed at times more like intimate enemies. Neither wanted to come in second in anything, and that included getting her driver's license.

Abandoning the double debris that accumulated every year on their birthday, I grabbed my purse and a magazine, while the girls flung themselves into our minivan, urging me to hurry up. As we drove to the Department of Motor Vehicles in South Yarmouth, I shot up a silent prayer as I considered the implications of the step we were about to take:

"Dear Lord, help us! Two overconfident teenagers let loose on the roads, skyrocketing automobile insurance rates, one minivan with too many drivers . . . Father, help me find the humor in this situation!"

At the DMV I settled into an uncomfortable plastic chair with a magazine and watched the girls negotiate the lines of applicants together. When they reached the head of the line, I noticed that the usually efficient clerk seemed to be taking an unusually long time studying their paperwork. She glanced at the girls, looking from one to the other, and then returned her gaze to their applications. *What could be taking so long?* I wondered. *She has approved other permits in a fraction of the time she's kept Amber and Sarah waiting.* I closed my magazine and walked up to the counter.

"Are you their mother?" the clerk said with a frown.

"I sure am," I answered. *What had we done wrong? Had I failed to make sure the girls brought the right documents?* "What seems to be the problem? Is everything OK?"

"Oh, everything's in order," the clerk responded. She offered an embarrassed smile. "It's just that your daughters have the same address, same phone number, and same parents listed. It's all right here. And the same birth date: May 3, 1984."

Sarah turned to me anxiously, while Amber simply looked exasperated.

"Yes?" I responded cautiously.

"Well, I know it's really none of my business, but they have different last names!"

New Englanders are not known for inquiring into others' personal business, but it was obvious what she was thinking: *Twin girls with different fathers? Just how did you manage that?* I stared at her for a moment and then burst into laughter.

Eager to get on with it, Amber set the matter straight. "One of us is a foster," she explained.

The clerk examined brown-eyed, brunette Amber and then fair-haired Sarah. She stared again at me—the girls' blonde, blue-eyed mother. "Oh-h-h," the clerk said, nodding sympathetically at Amber. "Aren't you the lucky one?"

But it was Sarah—ward of the foster system and child of my heart—who had the last word. "We're both lucky," she said as their permits were approved.

We turned to leave, and I lagged a few steps behind as the girls hurried out to the van, sparring good-naturedly over which one should have the privilege of getting behind the wheel first. Tears suddenly formed in my eyes, surprising me. *No, I'm the lucky one*, I thought.

I could not give Amber a sister, but God had. Sarah needed a home, and God had one for her. Two unique young women born on the same day of the same month of the same year to different families, now living as sisters in the same home.

Remembering the clerk's confusion about their last names, I smiled. I should have told her the most important thing Amber and Sarah had in common: the same heavenly Father.

—*Maggie Wallem Rowe*

WHEN GOD BREAKS THROUGH

Paul wrote to the Galatians: "God has sent the Spirit of his Son into your hearts, and now you can call God your dear Father. Now you are no longer a slave but God's own child. And since you are his child, everything he has belongs to you" (Galatians 4:6–7, NLT).

All of us who belong to God have been born again and adopted into his family and become God's sons and daughters. As Christians we carry the faith legacy of all who have gone before us, from Abraham (the father of our faith) to King David to Jesus himself. We even have the rights and privileges as brothers and sisters of Christ—including the ability to say with Jesus, "Abba," the Hebrew word for "Daddy," when we come before God. As God's children, we share in the great treasures he has to offer: a personal relationship with his Son, forgiveness, and eternal life.

MY CHALLENGE

What does it mean to you to be adopted into God's family? Do you feel like his child or more like an orphan? Ephesians 1:3–14 provides a list of blessings we have because we are his: God has chosen us in Christ to be holy; he has showered us with his wonderful kindness, forgiven us our sins through the blood of his Son, provided us with all wisdom and understanding, and given us the Holy Spirit as his guarantee that we belong to him. As you read these verses and reflect on these blessings, select the one that is the most meaningful to you today.

5 THE BLIND SHALL SEE
Seeing Jesus When Life Goes Dark

"We are coming to the doorway. Watch your step."

"The guest booth is on your left. We need to veer to the right."

"Mr. Olson is coming to talk to you."

I'd never before seen the man who was walking toward the church building. But I knew the McCoys, the people he was walking between. Mr. and Mrs. McCoy were special people who had welcomed me with open arms a year earlier when I had come to the church as youth minister. They loved God, the church, and people, and they'd always encouraged me.

Now I learned the man in his 30s walking between the two was their oldest son, Donald, who'd recently moved in with them. I wanted to know Donald better, so a few days later I picked Donald up for lunch. Over pizza he told me his story.

Two years earlier he'd started having sight problems. At first he thought it was night blindness or something treatable. But it had turned out to be an incurable, debilitating disease.

"If you had told me two years ago that I would lose my eyesight and be at peace about it, I would have said you were crazy," Donald told me. "I would have lashed out at God, at life, and at anyone who tried to comfort me."

"How did you keep from getting angry?" I asked.

"Oh," said Donald, "I was angry. I cried many nights and asked God, 'Why me?' I was a basket case the first few months."

"What brought the change?" I queried.

"I began to think about all the people—saints and spiritual giants—who'd gone before me and who'd endured pain, misfortune, and crisis. Like Job. He was a righteous man. He was rich, and in Old Testament times that was a symbol of God's blessings. He had great health, a large and loving family, and a sterling character. He was one of the best men that ever lived. Then he lost everything. His life fell apart even though he was doing everything right.

"God convinced me about the heroes of the faith. Have you *really* read Hebrews 11?" he asked me.

"Well, yes," I replied. "The faith of Moses, Abraham, Joseph, and Enoch is admirable."

"Yeah, I'd read those stories," Donald said. "But then I got to the end of the chapter and the author of Hebrews talks about those who were tortured, flogged, chained, put in prison, stoned, sawed in two. Others were destitute, persecuted, and mistreated. 'The world was not worthy of them,' the Bible says. And God seemed to say, 'Does your blindness compare with the injustice that these people went through?' I was convicted."

Donald paused to sip his soda. Then he continued, "When David Livingstone returned to his native Scotland after 16 years as a missionary in Africa, his body was emaciated by fevers that had coursed through his body during the years of his service. He couldn't use his left arm because a lion had mangled it. But when he spoke to the students of Glasgow University, he said, 'Shall I tell you what sustained me during the hardships and loneliness of my exile? It was Christ's promise, "Lo, I am with you always, even unto the end."' Then he said, 'This is the word of a gentleman of the most strict and sacred honor.'

"If Job and the great people of faith and David Livingstone didn't escape suffering, how could I?" Donald stated.

Donald also brought up Helen Keller and the great blind hymnist Fanny Crosby, who wrote songs such as "To God Be the Glory," "Praise Him! Praise Him!" and Donald's favorite, "All the Way My Savior Leads Me." He quoted the first stanza to me:

> All the way my Savior leads me;
> What have I to ask beside?
> Can I doubt his tender mercy,
> Who thro' life has been my guide?
> Heav'nly peace, divinest comfort,
> Here by faith in him to dwell!
> For I know whate'er befall me,
> Jesus doeth all things well.

"If Jesus did all things well for Fanny Crosby and she was blind, then I realized God would do all things well in my blindness too," Donald said.

I was overwhelmed by Donald's perspective and his faith. Here was a man who had visited with God. As a result, his life had been touched, changed.

Donald took the worst life could throw at him and saw Jesus in it. He interpreted his loss of eyesight as God's way to get through to him.

Donald took the worst life could throw at him and saw Jesus in it.

"I began to realize that God was chiseling on the interior recesses of my life," Donald said. "I don't particularly like the process. Nothing is enjoyable about losing my vision, but through this I have come to see Jesus and to trust in him. And if blindness is what it took for me to come back to him, then I am glad it happened.

"I had to go blind before I could see Jesus," Donald told me. "I pray that what has happened to me will never happen to you . . . unless that's what it takes for you to see Jesus too."

—*Rick Ezell*

WHEN GOD BREAKS THROUGH

An experience such as losing sight could destroy most people, leaving them bitter. Donald chose to look at his experience with spiritual eyes. He chose to see Jesus in his blindness. The fact is we will face our share of debilitating issues of life. Life is at times cruel, unjust, and unmerciful. God wants us to see the momentary affliction as a way he can conform us to his Son. It takes a unique brand of faith to see God in those times. God offers us that faith through his Son, "The Spirit of the LORD is upon me, for he has anointed me to bring Good News to the poor. He has sent me to proclaim that captives will be released, that the blind will see, that the oppressed will be set free, and that the time of the LORD's favor has come" (Luke 4:18–19, NLT).

MY CHALLENGE

The next time you face one of life's disappointments—death, disease, or defeat—use the instance as a magnet to draw you to Jesus. Choose to look beyond the pain to see Jesus' presence. When calamity or accidents happen to God's children, we see them as tools to drive us to him.

At the Table of the King

Finding Christmas in an Unexpected Place

The apartment was stark with cold concrete walls musty with mold. A single orange light bulb hung from the ceiling. Musty grass mats were scattered on the floor; the smell of alcohol wafted in from the bars below. Although the calendar said it was Christmas Eve, it didn't seem like it that first night in our apartment when we were new missionaries in Japan.

My husband and I shivered despite the propane space heater, which provided the only warmth in the room. Both of us jumped as a train whistle blasted into our tiny living area. The pastor hadn't been kidding when he told us we'd be close to public transportation! We were just ten feet from the train station.

Slowly we unpacked our belongings, trying to shut out memories of glowing fireplaces and family gatherings where the Bible's story of the first Christmas was read aloud. My eyes were misty and I feigned busyness.

Just weeks before at our home church in America, we had shared our concerns about going to the mission field. We wept as we sang a song based on Philippians 3:8. The words had seemed easy then as we soared on the heights of a vision of pressing on to serve Christ.

Now, Colleen, stop feeling sorry for yourself. What did you expect? A palace? I scolded myself. *But on the other hand, something warmer and farther away from the train station would be nice.*

ALONG THE WAY

Arguing with myself was getting me nowhere, so I quickly brushed away those thoughts, determined to make the best of it. I grabbed an empty box, covered it with a towel, and arranged on it the Christmas cards that had come the day before with pictures of friends and family. A plate with a few cookies and oranges—leftovers from a Christmas party at a convalescent home—became the centerpiece. Though they seemed a pitiful substitute for the laden tables of past years, we sat carefully, like children pretending to have a tea party with the king.

We began to pray. We lifted up the names of those whose dear faces we saw in the pictures on our table. Friends had sent a photo of their newborn baby.

"Thank you, Lord," my husband began, "for coming to this earth as a baby." At that moment all pretense left, and we began to weep. The bubble of our grand image of ourselves as new missionaries burst.

And then Jesus came. As my husband said, "Thank you for coming as a baby," it was as if Jesus spoke to both of us, "Yes, I came as a baby, but right now I am coming to you in your loneliness." The orange light deepened, and a stillness of joy and peace filled the room. We could almost see beautiful robes and feel the touch of his hands on our heads, comforting us. Now we both cried unabashedly but this time with tears of joy.

We understood what Paul meant when he spoke about the "fellowship of his suffering." This was a sort of baptism for us. We never would have experienced such loneliness or isolation in the midst of prosperity and friends. We never would have experienced Jesus' presence as we did that lonely Christmas Eve in our bare apartment.

We also realized that we were blessed with a revelation of the true Spirit of Christmas—that the Lord left his heavenly home and comforts to come as a poor baby into a stable that probably wasn't any better than the apartment where we lived. That night we received the most wonderful Christmas gift of all—the gift of the kingly baby now glorified, wrapped in the brown paper of earthly discomfort.

We understood what Paul meant when he spoke about the "fellowship of his suffering."

—*Colleen Yang*

WHEN GOD BREAKS THROUGH

Sometimes we have to leave our comfort zone and venture into unknown territory before we experience God to a new degree. Being Jesus' disciple is not only about sacrifice or doctrine but also about Jesus meeting us and transforming our need into a glorious revelation of his presence. Once we experience that taste of his presence, we'll never be content with anything less. As Paul wrote while sitting in a prison cell in Rome:

> But whatever former things I had that might have been gains to me, I have come to consider as one combined loss for Christ's sake. Yes, furthermore, I count everything as loss compared to the possession of the priceless privilege—the overwhelming preciousness, the surpassing worth, and supreme advantage of knowing Christ Jesus my Lord and of progressively becoming more deeply and intimately acquainted with Him, of perceiving and recognizing and understanding him more fully and clearly.—Philippians 3:7–8, AMP

Sometimes God doesn't want to just whisk away the pain or loneliness of our circumstances but he wants to use them to draw us to himself. Then he can transform our circumstances into a revelation of the great and surpassing treasure of knowing him.

MY CHALLENGE

Think about a difficult time you've endured. If you are alone, imagine that the Lord is sitting next to you and holding your hand. What is he saying to you? How would you like him to meet you? Express that to him right now. What images of yourself do you need to release? The loneliness is real, but he can transform it into a peaceful solitude. Take some time to find him there. He is waiting.

7 A Boy for Brutus
Trusting God to Meet Our Needs

"Are you going to take my dog?" the boy asked, his voice quivering. He stood behind his mother with tears in his eyes. I looked away as she scooped him into her arms.

"Remember what I told you, Tommy? We're moving to a small apartment, and we can't take the dog. This nice lady will take him."

"But *why?*" he wailed.

I tried to control my emotions. I felt bad for Tommy and his mom. The older kids would miss Brutus, she told me, but he was Tommy's dog, so it was toughest for him.

Brutus was a beautiful golden retriever with liquid brown eyes and a coat the color of butterscotch pudding. All he had ever known was this family's love. I couldn't let him go to a shelter where row after row of caged animals paced back and forth, eyes pleading to be rescued from their concrete-and-wire existence.

Listening to Tommy's cries as I walked away with Brutus, I knew I was doing the right thing. So why did it feel so wrong?

Brutus and I settled into a daily routine. Every morning we walked in the neighborhood, and every night I shared popcorn or pieces of a bologna sandwich with him. He often made me laugh as he cocked his head and howled along when I sang.

I was content, but Brutus only seemed truly happy when we met children on our walks. Then his tail wagged, his ears perked up, and his step turned springy. When the kids played fetch with him or wrapped their arms around him, his mouth opened into a smile and his eyes danced. When the children left, his spirit drooped and his eyes clouded with sadness.

One night I sat on the floor with Brutus. I looked into his eyes and felt a connection that seemed beyond words. "I'm not supposed to keep you, am I?" I said aloud. The thought made me sad. I loved this dog. I scratched behind his ears. It would be easy to keep him, but was that the right thing to do?

"I need to find you a home with kids again, where you can chase them around the backyard and play tug-of-war with old socks. You miss resting your head on a boy's tummy when he watches television or curling up by his feet when he does his homework."

Brutus let out a long sigh and stretched out on the floor at my side. I knew I was doing all I could to make him happy. I gave him a home when he desperately needed one. But he needed something I couldn't give. It wasn't fair to keep him to myself without the companionship of children he so desperately craved.

"OK, Brutus," I whispered in his ear. "Let's find you a family." He licked my face and wagged his tail.

"God," I prayed, "you always provide just what we need. Please help me." Soon I felt a comfortable peace. Somehow I knew Brutus was destined to be a young boy's dog again.

A short time later I was walking Brutus when three young girls ran out of a house.

"Your dog is so beautiful," the youngest girl said, kneeling and stroking Brutus' head. "We want a dog just like him!"

I told her I was looking for a home for Brutus. "Do you girls have a brother?"

"No," the girls said.

"Can you wait here while I go get my dad?" asked the youngest. "Please, please?"

I was dumbfounded. This couldn't be right. This family had only daughters. As I waited, the older girls continued to pet Brutus, whose tail continued wagging.

"My dad is busy," the little girl said when she returned, "but can he talk to you later?"

That evening the father came over. "I've wanted a golden retriever for the kids," he said, "but I'm not sure how the girls will adjust to a pet. Can I take Brutus for a week to decide if it will work out?"

At the end of the week, the father walked back up the sidewalk with Brutus on his leash. "I have bad news," he said. "A dog is more responsibility than the girls thought, and they aren't ready for it. I'm sorry, but I have to give Brutus back."

I took Brutus into the house. His eyes were sadder now than before. I needed to find him a home with children and quickly.

I looked at Brutus and silently prayed, *OK, now what?* That's when the idea came to place an ad in our community paper. While I was at work, my sister would show the dog to any callers. The day after the paper was circulated, my sister called to say a family was on their way to see Brutus, and she would let them in. As the next hour dragged by, I was torn between wanting what was best for Brutus and not wanting to give him up.

Then the phone rang again.

"B. J., the family is here—a mom and dad with their four children. They seem really nice, and they want to take Brutus with them."

"I haven't even said goodbye!" I told her, a little stunned by the suddenness.

"Well, they really like him. What do you want to do?" my sister gently pressed.

> *His eyes were sadder now than before. I needed to find him a home with children— quickly.*

"Tell them they can take him, but get their address and phone number," I said. "Tell them I want to come by tomorrow before work to say goodbye."

When I came home that night, I gathered Brutus' extra leash and toys to deliver the next day. My eyes were filled with tears. In the morning I called the Millers' house at 7:30 sharp. "I hope I didn't wake you."

"With a little baby and youngsters to get ready for school, this is definitely not too early. Come on over," Mrs. Miller said.

On the way, I felt excited. Brutus was with children again! Even though I would miss him, I knew he would be happy. I parked in front of the ranch-style home and walked to the door. Through the kitchen window, I saw a lot of activity—sandwiches being assembled for school lunches, a little girl laughing and eating breakfast, and Mrs. Miller watching a baby in her swing.

"Come on in, B. J.," she invited when I knocked.

"Thank you for letting me come to say goodbye," I said.

"No problem. I understand. Brutus is in the family room with Dan."

We walked down the hall. In the family room I saw well-worn furniture, a television set in the corner, and a pet door leading to a grassy backyard with a swing set and huge trees. A teenage boy knelt next to Brutus.

"Hello, Brutus," I said. He raised his head and wagged his tail. He walked to me, and I petted his silky coat. I looked for the sadness that used to be in those liquid brown eyes, but now I only saw contentment.

"This is our son, Dan," Mrs. Miller said. "Dan is a big help to me with the younger children, and he's always doing helpful chores for the neighbors. We've decided that Brutus will be Dan's dog. We've always wanted a golden retriever," she added.

I had only been a stepping-stone in this dog's journey through life. Now Brutus had a family again and best of all, a boy of his very own.

—B. J. Taylor

When God Breaks Through

God always provides just what we need—if we take time to see his hand in our daily situations. We can trust that God will always meet our needs. That doesn't mean he will always give us what we want, but we can have confidence, as did Paul, that "this same God who takes care of me will supply all your needs from his glorious riches, which have been given to us in Christ Jesus" (Philippians 4:19, NLT). As we trust God to provide what we *need*, we will discover that our attitudes and perspective about what we *want* will change.

My Challenge

Make a list of what you want right now in a specific situation. Take a moment to reflect on that list and then pray. Now make a list of what you need to cope in that situation. Ask God to change your attitude and perspective as you trust him to supply your needs.

8 BACKPACKER IN THE RAIN

Extending Acts of Mercy to Others

"It's about to start raining. Do you want to get indoors?" I asked the young man. "Come over to my house and have lunch."

I'd noticed him when I dashed into the post office to buy some stamps. He stood on the curb looking as if he'd just stepped off a bus and wasn't sure of his next move. He leaned over his backpack, adjusting straps and snaps, and then looked up at the sky, clouds black and rolling.

As a certified member of the international brotherhood of wandering backpackers, I knew what it felt like to be standing under an imminent rain cloud without a place to go for shelter. Although inviting a stranger home for lunch isn't an action I'd usually recommend, I sensed it was the right thing to do in this case. A wanderer myself, and a student at Princeton, I certainly didn't have much for him to steal, and I was used to taking care of myself.

He studied me and then said, "Ahh! Mmm, yes. Thank you. Please, I will."

"Then let's go, fast!" I said and ran to my car parked half a block away. He ran too, with the huge backpack slung over his shoulder. We threw it in the back and collapsed into the front seat. As we slammed the doors, the storm hit with all its fury.

You haven't seen an electrical storm until you've seen one over Princeton. The lightning nearly makes you jump out of your skin, and the thunder that follows microseconds later is like an Abrams tank firing at you from 15 feet away. We sat in my old car for a minute and just watched the water cascading. We couldn't see more than 10 feet beyond the windshield.

Having traveled all over with a backpack for many years, I had an idea what the guy thought as he sat in my dry car, looking at where he'd stood moments before.

Sure enough, he looked at me somewhat astonished. "*Danke!* Thank you, again." He couldn't believe his luck.

He told me his story as I drove: A musician from Germany, he had come to the States to explore for a month. He'd been in America for five days, the first four in New York City. His misadventures there had not led him to expect the hospitality I was giving him.

By the time we reached my apartment, the rain had slowed enough for us to dash indoors. I already had food ready to put on the stove. Two friends were supposed to lunch with me that day, but they'd called at the last minute to say they couldn't come. That's when I'd decided to go get the stamps before I fixed lunch. In a skillet I'd placed dark sausages, covered by a layer of onions, potatoes, and cabbage and topped by a couple of eggs.

His misadventures in New York City had not led him to expect the hospitality I was giving him.

"You eat sausages here?" my new friend, Wolfhart, asked, somewhat surprised. He looked delighted as he settled into a comfortable chair and surveyed my apartment.

"Sometimes," I replied. "Today, yes. For you," I added, and we both laughed.

While the sausages and potatoes cooked, I went to my stereo and started Mozart's *Quartet in F* for four clarinets, something I've always liked. Then I headed back to the kitchen to turn the sausages over.

"That is Mozart!" Wolfhart said. "It is his, um, quartet, no? For clarinets?"

"Wow. That's pretty good. You recognized it after only a few measures."

"No, no," he sputtered, "but
is my favorite. My favorite! I am
clarinetist in Berlin Orchestra.
You know?"

Not only had he been rescued
from the rain just in the nick of
time, but he also was going to have
sausages and potatoes for lunch,
and the music playing for him in
his unexpectedly dry sanctuary
was his very favorite piece.

That afternoon and into the night we talked about deep matters—
matters of history, matters of culture, matters of the soul. I don't think
I have ever so poignantly articulated the significance of Jesus Christ's
resurrection as I heard myself doing that night. Wolfhart understood
perfectly too. I have no doubt that Jesus was with us in my apartment, and
that Wolfhart knew it too.

—Gene Smillie

When God Breaks Through

Whenever we extend ourselves and offer others hospitality, a warm smile, an encouraging word, we can be assured not only is Jesus with us, but it is also as if we are offering Jesus himself a glass of water, shelter, or a hot meal. As Jesus told his disciples, "For I was hungry, and you fed me. I was thirsty, and you gave me a drink. I was a stranger, and you invited me into your home" (Matthew 25:35, NLT). Though most of us will not invite strangers off the street into our homes, we can perform numerous acts of mercy each day if only we keep our eyes open and our spirits willing.

My Challenge

Reflect upon the past 24 or 48 hours. What opportunities were available for you to perform an act of mercy to another person? Think about how you responded in each situation. How does your attitude change as you realize that Jesus not only orchestrated these opportunities for you but also is present as you freely give?

9 A MOTHER'S DAY FLOWER

Finding Worth in God's Eyes

Spring arrived with a mixture of hope and helplessness. My tulips and daffodils were up, but my spirits were down. Wisconsin was living up to its reputation of having unpredictable weather. I knew my flowers would probably survive a short frost, but the fickleness of the season seemed to reflect a fluctuating chill and thaw in my soul that I wasn't so sure I'd survive.

My three children were almost grown. My oldest son was serving in the military, and my heart vacillated between pride and worry. My middle child could hardly wait to leave high school. My youngest and only daughter was entering womanhood and the strain between us seemed natural but painful. As my children grew, I felt my central purpose shrinking. They weren't my children anymore—they were my grown-ups.

That year, Mother's Day seemed an empty formality. What was the point?

So that year Mother's Day seemed an empty formality. What was the point? Why be called Mom if my kids no longer really needed me?

On Mother's Day all three children accompanied me to church. My husband, Neil, was the pastor of a small country church with a number of quaint traditions. Mother's Day always received special treatment. During the children's sermon, Neil asked the children to distribute flowers to all the moms in the congregation. Children ran back and forth, seeking candidates for motherhood. Some of their guesses added humor to the gestures of honor.

I sat in the middle of a pew with my three big kids between the aisle and me, but a sweet little imp passing out flowers spotted me and handed over a bloom. That little gift provoked a decision in my heart. There in that pew, I set aside the confused feelings I had struggled with for weeks and let myself bask in the glow of being a mom.

I'm a mom, and even if my role is changing, my kids still—and will always— need me to be their mom.

My reverie was interrupted by a sudden stillness. I looked up to see my oldest son walking down the aisle toward his dad, who was still sorting and distributing flowers. Everyone in the place seemed to lock eyes on this young man whom most of them had watched grow up. My son selected a flower from his dad, turned, and walked back up the aisle toward me. Leaning over his siblings he offered me the flower and swept me up off my seat with a strong hug and kiss.

I cried. Because I decided to stop struggling with my validity as a mother, I could relish the flower as a wonderful and genuine gift of love and honor. God might have whispered the idea in my son's ear as he sat there that Mother's Day. Perhaps not. But my heart fills with gratitude every time I remember that day.

—Sherrie W. as told to Neil Wilson

WHEN GOD BREAKS THROUGH

Sometimes we must take our eyes off ourselves before we can receive God's love and affirmation. But he is always there, waiting for us to look at him. Jesus assures us of his Father's steadfast love for us and of our worth in his eyes with these words, "And if God cares so wonderfully for flowers that are here today and gone tomorrow, won't he more surely care for you? You have so little faith!" (Matthew 6:30, NLT).

MY CHALLENGE

When have you felt unappreciated, ignored, or unsure of your role and worth? How does Matthew 6:28–30 speak to you about the Father's love for you?

10 RAISING ASHLEY
Praying Through Life's Challenges

Oh, Lord, it's asking a lot for me to be a mother again. I'm 82 years old!

But I didn't have a choice. My son had been raising his 11-year-old, Ashley, alone. But then he died, and Ashley's mom couldn't care for her.

My blonde granddaughter looked so much like her father. When he was young, her father used to test the limits, pushing as hard as he could before I put my foot down. I suspected this sweet child was much like her father. Taking her into my home, I'd have to pray extra hard, that was for sure.

"Ashley, you'll come and live with me," I told her. "You'll have to follow my rules—like doing your homework, getting up on time for school, and coming to church with me every Sunday."

"I know, Nana," Ashley said. "And I can bring the dogs, right?"

I'd forgotten about Ashley's dogs, Scorpio and Bogey—a King Charles spaniel and a wirehaired schnauzer. And my son's dog, Buddy, was a cocker spaniel. I didn't want three dogs in my small house. But what could I say?

"Yes, Ashley, the dogs too."

We moved in Ashley's belongings. As soon as the dogs came in the door, I knew I'd have a lot less peace and quiet.

When Ashley came in my door, all my expectations about life flew out the windows! My mornings had always been filled with quiet, lingering moments over a big cup of coffee. That gentle start to my day soon ended with Ashley's alarm exploding at 6 a.m.

"Don't hit that snooze button again!" I yelled down the hall nearly every day. "Get up and get ready for school." We soon developed a routine of having breakfast together before I drove Ashley to school.

One morning Ashley emerged from her bedroom dressed unacceptably.

"Ashley, you know the school requires you to wear a shirt with at least a cap sleeve," I scolded. "No sleeveless tops, no spaghetti straps."

"So many rules! Why can't I just do what I want?" Ashley yelled as she stomped back into her room.

Lord, this child is testing my patience. And so early in the morning too.

Sixth grade was hard for Ashley with different classrooms and teachers for each subject and gym classes. She was not adjusting well. After a parent/teacher conference, I sat with Ashley at the kitchen table. "What's up with your behavior at school? The teachers tell me you're not doing as well as you could."

"School is lame. It's all the teachers' faults," Ashley said. "They don't write the assignments on the board, and I can't remember what my homework is. It's just too hard."

God, this girl has been through so much. Help me to help her.

"You have to pay attention in class, Ashley," I said with what I hoped was an encouraging tone. "I know you're just not listening like you should be. You're a smart girl, and you need to apply yourself."

God, I prayed, *this girl has been through so much. Help me to help her.*

"Ashley, I'm going to give it to you straight," I announced. She raised her eyes to my face. "I feel bad for you. You've been through a lot, but that does not give you leeway to misbehave or not study. I'm here for you and will make things as right as I can. But you do not have an excuse to do things you shouldn't do."

That night I lay in bed wondering, *Am I doing the right thing, Lord? It feels like all I do is dole out discipline.*

Ashley was in her room with the dogs. The house was so quiet I could hear myself breathing. Then I heard an answer to my prayer. Soft. Comforting. Like it came from Jesus himself. *Just do your best. That's all I ask. And have faith.*

I went to sleep with peace in my heart.

Our problems didn't disappear the next day. We continued butting heads. Like most 11-year-olds, Ashley thought she knew everything. One of her hardest school subjects was math. "I have a friend at church who's a retired teacher," I told her. "Let's ask him to help you."

"I don't need a tutor," Ashley shot back. "I can figure it out on my own."

"Well, that's just not working, young lady, so we're going to ask him to give you some lessons," I firmly told her.

"Whatever," Ashley said as she turned and left the room.

Twice a week we met with the tutor, and after a while Ashley's math grade started to improve. But it was still a struggle. She came home one day with a D on a test. "Nana, I just don't get this stuff!"

"I know, sweetheart," I tried to console her. "Life isn't always easy, but let's keep trying."

One day, after a particularly difficult discussion over what Ashley could watch on television, I wondered if this was just too much for both of us. I hadn't seen Ashley smile much lately. We used to have fun watching movies and eating popcorn together on weekend sleepovers. Again I turned to prayer and asked God to show me a way to have fun with my granddaughter.

One of the constants in our lives was church. We learned about a church camp in the mountains and scraped together the money for Ashley to go. Then the church asked me to come along as the camp nurse since I had kept my nursing license current after retiring. *Lord, thank you for giving us something fun we can do together,* I prayed.

Ashley bunked in the girls' dorm, and I had my own little room in the first aid cabin. Ashley came to sit with me sometimes, and one night she said, "Nana, thanks for bringing me here." She chattered on about what fun she'd had that day, and I listened with delight.

Prayer continued to sustain me. I prayed over everything and found nonpreachy ways to encourage my granddaughter to learn to walk closely with God.

Ashley worked at a pet store bathing, brushing, walking, and feeding the dogs. "There's a dog adoption fair this weekend. I want to work the booth both Saturday and Sunday," she told me one week. "Is that OK? So many dogs need a home and people to love them. For some, the fair is their only hope. Please?"

I took a long moment to think. Should I let her skip a Sunday service?

Ashley sat on the sofa with Bogey on one side of her and Scorpio on the other. Buddy was on the floor nestled at my feet. I cleared my throat.

"Yes, you can work the dog adoption fair both days this weekend." Then I added with a smile, "But don't make a habit of missing church."

"Thanks, Nana," Ashley said. She planted a kiss on my cheek before running out the door.

I thought about that night when I heard Jesus direct me with "Just do your best. That's all I ask. And have faith."

Running Ashley to everything she's involved in keeps me going. To say I get tired is an understatement, but each day I pray for strength, and God provides it. When things get tough, I've learned not to get upset—I think it through, ask God for help, and follow through.

Maybe this isn't the life I thought I'd be living, but it's the life God has planned for me. And I am thankful.

—*Ulla C. as told to B. J. Taylor*

WHEN GOD BREAKS THROUGH

When we face a new challenge, we can complain or shirk the responsibility. Or we can know and tap into the power of God's immeasurable strength through prayer. In 1 Thessalonians 5:17, Paul admonishes us to "always keep on praying" (TLB)—four simple words that many of us find very challenging. We might amend that statement to fit our actions: "keep on worrying"; "keep on doubting"; "keep on relying on our own strength." But some of life's challenges are beyond our alleged strength. That's why the invitation to "keep on praying" is such a comfort as Ulla attests. God breaks through our worry and doubt with a solid reminder that he's always there ready to offer help. Prayer isn't a passive, I'll-just-pass-the-buck response to life's challenges. Prayer is where you seek and gain the wisdom, courage, and strength to act.

MY CHALLENGE

What is your formula when facing a challenge? Do you pray first or not until you've exhausted every other resource? If prayer is the last thing on your list, consider God's ability to sustain you. We burn out needlessly because we don't ask for help. Note Ulla's formula: "I think it through, ask God for help, and follow through." Make Ulla's formula yours. What do you need to think through? Are you willing to ask God for help? If so, how will you follow through when he answers?

11 WHOM DO YOU TRUST?

Discovering God's Perfect Plan

"Who do you trust, Heidi?" my husband asked with a tender smile. He seemed to read the fear in my heart as I pushed through the contraction. Despite the team of physicians at my bedside in one of the best hospitals in Texas, I was scared. I was frightened by what lay ahead and, as much as I hated to admit it, I was afraid of our little baby himself.

My husband squeezed my hand and gently repeated, "Who do you trust, Heidi?"

His words were what I needed to hear. "I trust in God," I told him.

I'd first said those words more than four months earlier when I got the call. It couldn't have come at a worse time. I barely heard the phone ring over the swoosh of packing tape being stretched over boxes and the shouts of movers' voices. I tripped over the contents of my bedroom closet, now strewn across the floor, in my hurry to answer the phone.

"The results from your amniocentesis have come back," my doctor told me. *"Unfortunately your baby has Down syndrome."*

"The results from your amniocentesis have come back," my doctor told me. "Unfortunately your baby has Down syndrome."

Tears rolled down my cheeks and I whispered the words that felt like a curse to my husband who stood beside me.

"You will have to decide if you want to continue this pregnancy," the doctor continued.

I trust in God, my heart whispered.

With confidence from deep within I replied calmly, "We will continue this pregnancy. God has given me this baby."

The trauma of moving to Texas for our first Air Force assignment suddenly paled next to the grief of not having a perfect baby. And I would have more sorrow: Tests showed that our son also had a heart defect— holes in the upper and lower chambers of his heart and blockage of the pulmonary artery. Without open-heart surgery to repair this defect after his birth, he would die.

I sank into a dark period of grief and mourning. Some might call it depression. I called it the "slimy pit" that David wrote about in Psalm 40.

I also entered a time of fervent prayer. I prayed for the baby in my womb like never before. I prayed early in the morning when I awoke, while doing household chores, while taking care of my daughter, and in the middle of the night when I woke from a fitful slumber. I enlisted the prayer support from everyone I knew—and everyone they knew. I pleaded with God to take away the Down syndrome and to heal our baby's heart.

One afternoon a neighbor knocked on our door. She said God had impressed on her that I would have a testimony of victory at the end of this ordeal. She also believed that in his time, God would heal our baby.

"I don't think I have enough faith," I said.

"God will give you the gift of faith as a result of what you're about to experience," she reassured me.

I was surprised to discover that she was right.

Who do you trust, Heidi? the Holy Spirit whispered to me during those bitter days.

I trust in God, I replied, wondering if I really did trust him fully.

On December 15, 2004, I met Samuel David Spencer for the first time face-to-face. He was so beautiful. So perfect. He didn't look like I had expected. He looked like a perfect newborn.

My husband and I enjoyed our first day with our baby so much that I almost doubted that he had a heart condition. The next day, however, Sam turned slightly blue. He was immediately transferred to the Neonatal Intensive Care Unit, where we camped out by his bedside for four weeks. Christmas was approaching. I wanted to pummel the carolers in the cafeteria who sang, "Have a holly, jolly Christmas . . ." My baby was fighting for his life.

Test results confirmed Down syndrome, and despite valiant efforts by the medical staff, Samuel continued to decline. His heart surgery would need to be performed sooner rather than later. We chose a doctor with a good reputation and in January flew with our son on an emergency medical flight to Children's Hospital in Miami.

As Samuel lay in the operating room just barely alive, the Holy Spirit spoke one more time: *Who do you trust, Heidi?*

I trust in God.

I had no one else to trust but God himself.

After six agonizing hours the smiling surgeon came out from the operating room and announced the success of the procedure. We cried. We jumped up and down. We knelt in humble gratitude to a God who still performed miracles.

God did give me a perfect child. Samuel was "wonderfully made" by a wonderful God, who formed his body and mind exactly as he saw fit. Nothing could be more perfect than that.

—Heidi Spencer

WHEN GOD BREAKS THROUGH

When distressing things happen in life, it's natural to give in to bitterness and resentfulness over the situation—to embrace a "Why me?" mindset.

Instead of succumbing to human nature, Heidi dealt with her emotions and listened to the quiet voice inside her heart telling her to trust the one who knew her best. Only when she released her fears and doubts and accepted the perfection of God's plan for Samuel and for her family did Heidi experience God's peace in her situation.

God did not give her an explanation. He did not answer her "Why me?" Nor did he change her circumstances. Instead God assured Heidi of his love, his presence, and his goodness. She could echo David's unwavering confidence in God: "For in the day of trouble he will keep me safe in his dwelling, he will hide me in the shelter of his tabernacle and set me high upon a rock" (Psalm 27:5, NIV).

MY CHALLENGE

Write down three questions you have for God. In which of those situations do you feel God asks you to trust him no matter what? If you find it difficult to accept God's plan for you right now, confide in a close friend or your pastor. Ask that person to pray for you and with you as you work through your feelings.

---

12 THE WORRY STONE
Finding God's Answer to Worry

"Hey, Mom! I got something for you," my teenage son announced as he banged the kitchen door behind him. "It's just what you need!"

I bit my tongue. *What I need is to know if you're going to be late,* I silently scolded my son. *And I need to know you're not bleeding in a ditch somewhere. That's all I need.*

I kept my thoughts to myself and took the small white box Rex shoved toward me. As my irritation at his lateness diminished, my curiosity grew. I noticed the mischievous smile on my son's face as I started to open the mysterious box, and I prepared my nerves for something to jump out at me.

Nothing jumped. Inside the box was a small rock, round, smooth, and cool. Why would a 16-year-old give his mom a rock?

Rex laughed and pointed to a small paper that accompanied the rock: "This is a worry stone. When you are tense, just take out this stone and rub it. Soon all your worries will disappear into thin air."

"Thanks, I think," I said. "I guess you know your mom pretty well."

"Oh, yeah," he answered. "You do enough worrying for everybody in this family. I don't know how any of us would survive without your worrying about every little thing we do or don't do."

I knew Rex was teasing, but his words held a lot of truth. I do tend to worry. I worry about things that have already happened. I even suffer from retroactive worry—concern that someone was offended or hurt by what I did or said. Or I worry about whether I did enough to help or I said the right thing.

And then there are the what-ifs. What if my sons go on a camping trip and their boat capsizes—can they swim well enough to save themselves? What if the church doesn't have enough money to keep the school going and my husband loses his teaching job? What if he can't find another one and we have to move?

Rubbing a smooth stone may feel good, but it couldn't take away my worries. Still, I kept the worry stone on my desk to remind me to worry less and trust God more. After some time the stone was misplaced, and I forgot about it.

And then there are the what-ifs. What if my sons go on a camping trip and their boat capsizes?

Rex and his brother grew up healthy and happy—they didn't end up in a ditch bleeding. They did well academically and went on to college and jobs. The school didn't close and my husband kept teaching for many years. My worrying didn't influence any of these outcomes whatsoever.

Our life wasn't always smooth sailing. We definitely experienced ups and downs, including a severe accident. But my worrying or not worrying didn't stop the bad things from occurring or make the good things happen.

Both sons married wonderful Christian women—even though I sometimes worried that they would never find the right person. And then there were grandchildren—a whole new generation to fret about.

The grandchildren stayed with me while their parents worked, and it was like having another family—wonderful! I did worry that they would fall off the slide or that their sniffles were something worse than a cold. But I congratulated myself on being more mature and relaxed with these kids than I had been with my own. I had learned that most of the things I worried about never happened.

I thought about the long-gone worry stone one day when I was with my four-year-old grandson, Matthew—Rex's youngest son. Matthew fussed about staying with me that day. He wanted to go home and play with a new toy he'd forgotten to bring to my house.

"Matthew, no one is at your house," I said. "Mom and Dad are both at work. And I can't stay at your house because I need to do some work here. So you will just have to wait until later to go home."

"Well, I could go home and stay by myself," Matthew said.

"Wouldn't you be scared and worried that something bad could happen if you were all alone?"

Matthew gave me a four-year-old's most serious look. "Grammy, I wouldn't be worried or scared. God is always with me—he would take care of me."

It was as if Rex were standing before me, 25 years earlier, telling me that I worried too much.

Matthew didn't get to go home alone. But he did teach his grandma a very important lesson that day.

—Jeanette Dall

WHEN GOD BREAKS THROUGH

At one time or another, perhaps all of us have wished we could do something like rub a worry stone and see our fears disappear. Worry doesn't provide any benefits; it robs us of our sleep and our health and reduces our ability to trust God. No wonder Jesus plainly tells us:

> Do not worry about your life, what you will eat or drink; or about your body, what you will wear. Is not life more important than food, and the body more important than clothes? Look at the birds of the air; they do not sow or reap or store away in barns, and yet your heavenly Father feeds them. Are you not much more valuable than they? Who of you by worrying can add a single hour to his life?—Matthew 6:25–27, NIV

So what is the antidote to worry? Not rubbing a stone but giving those worries to God and trusting that he will indeed take care of us.

MY CHALLENGE

Read the rest of Jesus' teaching on worry in Matthew 6:31–34 (NIV):

> So do not worry, saying, "What shall we eat?" or "What shall we drink?" or "What shall we wear?" For the pagans run after all these things, and your heavenly Father knows that you need them. But seek first his kingdom and his righteousness, and all these things will be given to you as well. Therefore do not worry about tomorrow, for tomorrow will worry about itself. Each day has enough trouble of its own.

In what areas of your life do you worry most? How might you choose to seek God first in those areas?

ALONG THE WAY

13 STAR STRUCK

*Finding God's Truth
in Unlikely Places*

*Forty yapping sixth graders and one blaring movie speaker above my seat on
the bus. So this is what it's like to chaperone the spring sixth-grade field trip!*

I laughed, turned off my cell phone, and changed my plans to catch up
on phone calls while the bus drove into the city. I didn't really have time for
this, but my son, Ryan, had volunteered me and I didn't want to
disappoint him.

Shouting over the din, I tried to talk with my son's teachers until we
arrived at the Museum of Natural History. I noticed several other buses
unloading excited kids who appeared eager to experience all the museum
could offer. Little did we realize that we'd experience a population explosion
of elementary school children. Just our luck—the day turned out to be one
of the museum's busiest days. I spent the first couple of hours doing constant
head counts to make sure all nine in my group were present, while keeping up
with the school's science teacher who was the fastest walker I had ever seen.

After lunch we were scheduled to view the planetarium show. The
entire sixth grade proceeded through the doors of the planetarium like so
many cattle.

"If anyone talks during the show, I won't ask you to leave," droned the
woman in charge of the planetarium. "I'll ask your entire group to leave."

The lights went down and the dome lit with stars. A famous actor's voice explained that planet Earth was formed billions of years ago by a cosmic collision.

Wait! What about God's awesome design and attention to detail in speaking our world into existence?

Maternal instinct took over and I slid over to whisper in my son's ear, "You know what you are hearing isn't true." He grimaced. I guess I was lucky no one saw me talking. I shudder to envision Ryan's entire class being thrown out because his mom couldn't keep quiet.

I began to think more deeply as the planetarium show continued—a veritable roller coaster of awareness. Even when facts were interpreted in a non-biblical way, I was still humbled by those facts and the majesty of Almighty God. But while he was big enough to create an astounding universe, I realized he was intimate enough to care about the smallest details of my life.

Wait! What about God's awesome design and attention to detail in speaking our world into existence?

As the voice continued booming and the scenes on the ceiling changed, I considered my recent rash of concerns. I could be thankful we faced nothing major, just the normal spate of trials. But I'd become so weary of them at times I'd wondered if God had become weary of my children and me too.

Now, contemplating him, how could I doubt that he was working all things together for my good? Were the struggles I faced raising three children by myself more than God could handle? Could anyone want better for my family than God? The painfully obvious answers seemed to take on new meaning for me because of those moments in the planetarium.

Suddenly the lights came on, and we were told where to exit. I spent the rest of the day at the museum with a grateful heart. Leave it to God to reveal himself in the least likely place on the least likely day I could have imagined!

—*Jill Noelle Greer*

WHEN GOD BREAKS THROUGH

> The heavens tell of the glory of God.
> The skies display his marvelous craftsmanship.
> Day after day they continue to speak;
> night after night they make him known.
> They speak without a sound or a word;
> their voice is silent in the skies;
> yet their message has gone out to all the earth,
> and their words to all the world.
> The sun lives in the heavens
> where God placed it. (Psalm 19:1–4, NLT)

Since the heavens tell of God's glory, all we need to do to confirm God's greatness is to gaze at the grandeur of the night sky or examine the exquisite beauty of the flowers in our garden or listen to the voices of the birds that come into our yard. God's goodness, his magnificent creativity, and ultimately his steadfast love for us are on display before us all day, every day. What other response can we offer but our heartfelt thanks and our awe for such majesty?

MY CHALLENGE

Take a few moments tonight to view the night sky. Allow your thoughts to focus on God and his incredible handiwork. Let the heavens tell you about God's glory and his marvelous craftsmanship.

14 BEAUTIFUL BUTTERFLY
Learning About God's Compassion

I watched the young girl approach, each step an effort. One leg flailed unsteadily while the other dragged behind. Her arms and hands were also unruly as she hobbled across the rec room on the arm of an orphanage caretaker. The pair was definitely headed in my direction. The caretaker plopped the girl next to me. I squirmed.

What am I supposed to do? I wondered. *I can't speak Chinese, and I don't even know if she can speak!*

She looked about 12 and appeared to be cheerful despite her cerebral palsy. Her jet-black hair formed two ponytails, and long, feathery bangs almost hid her bright, almond-shaped eyes. She seemed unaware that she lived in a world where people cared little for imperfect children—especially girls.

I sat there stiffly. *Why is this so difficult? She's no different from any other orphan, yearning to be loved.*

Still I wondered if I were capable of such love. I had traveled to China with a ministry that provides new shoes for needy children. The trip was about more than shoes, of course; it was about saying "Jesus loves you" through our gifts and the time we spent with the children. I questioned how we could really have an impact in only one afternoon, especially since we and the children spoke different languages.

I prayed for the Holy Spirit to be in control.

What do I do now, Lord? How do I love this girl for you?

Smiling, the young girl reached out to me. Still I hesitated to hug her. Instead I pulled out my digital camera and took her picture. I pointed to her image on the small screen, and delight danced in her eyes as she saw herself.

"Let's take one of both of us," I said. I leaned close to her and held the camera in front of us. This time she pointed to me, then to herself, when she saw our picture. Her smile was worth a million words. She held my hand as if to keep me close to her.

Together we made and colored a paper crown. I placed the crown on her head.

"You're a child of God," I said. "You deserve to wear a crown." But she took off the crown and placed it on my head!

What do I do now, Lord? How do I love this girl for you?

All the children received rings, and when I put hers on her finger, she jerked it off and tried to put it on mine.

Who was this child? What was her name? She could not tell me, but taking a pencil and a piece of paper, she printed her name: Yanoshi. Amazing! She understood and could do much more than I thought possible when we first met.

Yanoshi—the sound of her name was beautiful. *She* was beautiful, as beautiful as a butterfly. Like a butterfly, she fluttered into my life, silent and lovely, not demanding anything but offering her love. Despite my fear and self-consciousness, it was easy to respond to her and embrace her with love that flowed from deep within.

Before leaving for China I had prayed for the children I would meet, children just like Yanoshi, who had been abandoned by parents hoping for a perfect, healthy boy. I had prayed that the children I met would be able to see the light and love of Jesus in me.

But I was the one who found new light. I was the one who saw Jesus' love reflected in Yanoshi's dark eyes and her crooked smile.

At the end of the afternoon, I watched with a lump in my throat as Yanoshi hobbled away on the arm of her caretaker. I would not forget my beautiful butterfly.

—Barbara Collier

WHEN GOD BREAKS THROUGH

Our world is full of people who need compassion and mercy—those who cannot help themselves, those who need a second chance. As we demonstrate genuine care for others around us, we convey God's love and compassion to them.

Look for those empty, dark, chaotic places and ask God to use you to shine his light. Paul reminds us, "Be kind and compassionate to one another, forgiving each other, just as in Christ God forgave you" (Ephesians 4:32, NIV).

MY CHALLENGE

Who in your life has taught you the most about God's love and compassion for the hurting? What were the circumstances? What impact did that experience have on your life? What can you do today to offer that same love and compassion to someone else?

15 THE PATH TO RESTORATION
Working Through the Pain

Life as I knew it came to a screeching halt just as my car did.

Driving to work that sunny winter day, I approached an intersection. A driver to my right cut in front of me and stopped his car to turn left. It happened so quickly that our cars collided. *Wafoof!* The airbag exploded in my face, stunning me. Then I was jolted to reality by a sharp pain in my right ankle.

With whiplash and a fractured ankle, I began a new journey: two long months with no walking and no driving. My orthopedic surgeon emphasized that I was not to bear any weight on my ankle, and I strictly followed his orders. I became good friends with my crutches, my couch, and my pillow.

At my two-month checkup my doctor took one look at my still-purple right foot and exclaimed, "You show early signs of regional pain syndrome. Start working those muscles! The best thing you can do is bear weight on your foot. Let me see you walk."

"Right now? Without the boot and crutches?" I asked.

"Yes. Walk toward me."

Gingerly I stepped in his direction and felt a sharp pain in my ankle. The doctor sat me down again. "Does this hurt?" He took my foot and pushed my toes forward, then back.

"Yes!" I exclaimed.

"I'm not really concerned about the pain right now," he countered. "You need to work through the pain to make this foot better."

"Is there any chance of reinjuring my ankle at this point?"

"Not at all."

"If I'm not in danger of reinjuring it, I don't care about the pain either as long as I can walk!" I eagerly hobbled out of the doctor's office. I could walk! I could drive! I could finally ditch the boot and crutches!

Later that week while I was driving, I thought about relationships. Someone had just expressed interest in getting to know me better, and I instantly felt afraid.

A particularly difficult situation in high school had taught me that I couldn't trust others not to hurt me. So I tried to avoid pain in relationships. When I was hurt, I certainly couldn't let anyone know he or she had hurt me. So I learned to smile on the outside while resentment built inside, and I secretly blamed others for the pain they inflicted on me.

But lately God had been shifting my perspective away from "How has this person wronged me?" to "How do I need to change?"

Am I brave enough to give this one a shot? I wondered as I thought about this new possibility. Suddenly I envisioned a picture of my ankle and heard the doctor say, *I'm not really concerned about the pain right now. You need to work through the pain to make this foot better.*

Instantly I knew those words were meant for more than my ankle. The Holy Spirit strategically directed them at my heart.

A week later one of my close friends shared her concern that something inside me might be keeping me from embracing relationships. On Tuesday another friend said she felt I was distancing myself from her. Wednesday

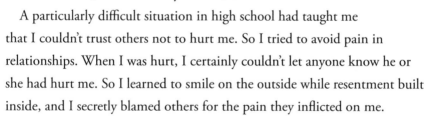

night another good friend shared that she felt I had put walls up in our friendship. Thursday, as I spoke with someone else, I was convicted of resentment I had harbored for a long time. On Friday someone else I've known for years told me that she had felt she was unimportant to me.

Am I brave enough to give this one a shot? I wondered as I thought about this new possibility.

I fought tears of sorrow. I had hurt people with my pride, selfishness, and unwillingness to trust. My heart agonized over the damage I had done.

At the same time, I was grateful that God had shown me through people he had placed in my life that I needed to keep working on my relationships. I am convinced that as I work through the pain to build new patterns of openness and trust, God will be right there.

—*Vicki Cairns*

WHEN GOD BREAKS THROUGH

Friendships are not easy. And the closer two people become, the more likely they are to clash at some time or another. Misunderstandings occur, we say things the wrong way, or emotions or fatigue interfere with our communication. Keeping relationships close and meaningful takes a lot of effort—practicing acceptance, grace, honesty, and forgiveness.

Sometimes when rifts occur in friendships, we're tempted to just put distance between ourselves and the friend, because that's the easy thing to do. But friendships, in the long run, keep us healthy and sane. They're worth working through the occasional pain to salvage. And when we work through the pain in a relationship, we find that the bonds of friendship are stronger than ever!

MY CHALLENGE

Proverbs 27:17 says, "As iron sharpens iron, a friend sharpens a friend" (NLT). Think about the relationships in your life. In what ways do friends sharpen or improve each other just by being friends? What strengths have some of your friends instilled or encouraged in your life? Do you have any relationships that need some maintenance to make them their best again? Are there friends with whom you need to practice acceptance, grace, honesty, or forgiveness?

16 THE INNKEEPER

Finding Goodness When You Least Expect It

"I'm sorry, Mr. Ezell, but your room has been given to someone else."

"What?" Daddy exclaimed.

We had arrived in downtown St. Louis later than we had planned, but we had a reservation.

"Sir, our policy states that if you don't arrive before six o'clock or inform us of your delay, we can give the room to someone else," the desk clerk said. "I'm sorry. Several conventions are in town, and many people need accommodations."

As a young boy of 12 or 13, I loved taking trips with Daddy in his white Chevy van, the first of its kind. Ambling down the highway I felt something almost magical as new places and possibilities opened before me. Yet I always felt secure because Daddy had traveled the road before.

"Don't you have even one available room?" Daddy inquired. "We'll take anything."

"No," the clerk stated. "We are full. You're not the first people we've had to turn away. I'm sorry."

Is he telling the truth? Maybe he doesn't like kids, I thought.

With us were my cousin Diane, who was three years older than me and like a sister, and my twin brother, Micky. Daddy owned a shoe store in northern Alabama and often traveled to Nashville, St. Louis, Atlanta, and Birmingham. He had a reputation for selling name-brand shoes at a fraction of their original cost and purchasing returns at rock-bottom prices. The hordes of shoppers who stood in line at Daddy's store every Thursday and Saturday attested to his niche in the shoe market.

"What about other hotels?" Daddy politely asked. "Are they also booked? Would any place else have available rooms?"

Daddy always had a confident demeanor. Nothing seemed to upset or frustrate him. He seemed to know that everything would work out.

"I don't think so, but let me check," the desk clerk replied.

We waited. The lobby was bright and big and offered a new world for a small-town boy to explore.

"What are we going to do?" I asked.

Daddy rarely became alarmed, but he looked perplexed.

The desk clerk returned. "No luck! All full! The conventions lured more people than expected. We do have rooms available for tomorrow night," he said.

"What are we going to do?" I asked.

Daddy rarely became alarmed, but he looked perplexed. I knew he was tired from driving all day and ready for a comfortable bed.

"I don't know," he said. "But we will be fine." He thought for a moment. "What if we sleep in the van? We have the blankets and pillows your mother packed. But . . . where?" Sleeping in a parked van on the streets of St. Louis wouldn't be safe.

He led us away toward the door.

"Sir," the desk clerk called out. "I have a suggestion. Hotel policy will not allow you to park overnight in the hotel garage since you are not a guest. But I can let you have my parking space in the employee section located just below the lobby. A door is near in case of an emergency, and the security guard will be close by. You are welcome to use the restrooms. I know this isn't much, but it's the best I have to offer. If you want to park there, the space is yours."

Daddy accepted the kind man's offer. I'm sure he thought that these arrangements were the best we would find at such a late hour.

That night we had the time of our lives camping out in the employee section of that parking garage. The accommodations were adequate, and we slept in peace.

Maybe it was from Daddy that I learned to look for the "Jesus moment" in the goodness of other people and circumstances working in my favor.

—*Rick Ezell*

WHEN GOD BREAKS THROUGH

Sometimes God has already provided the resources for our needs; we just need to see them and use them. At other times he works through others' generosity and compassion. Receiving someone else's compassionate act reminds us that God always goes before us, as he promised. The young man at the hotel may not have realized it, but he was doing exactly what God would have wanted him to do. God told his people through the prophet Isaiah, "I want you to share your food with the hungry and to welcome poor wanderers into your homes. Give clothes to those who need them, and do not hide from relatives who need your help. If you do these things, your salvation will come like the dawn. Yes, your healing will come quickly. Your godliness will lead you forward, and the glory of the Lord will protect you from behind" (Isaiah 58:7–8, NLT). It would have been easy for Rick's dad to have been angry at the hotel clerk and at God. Instead, he was willing to let God provide in a different way—a parking space and an unforgettable experience.

MY CHALLENGE

As room was found for Joseph and Mary in the barn beside the inn, so room was found for Rick and his family in the employee parking lot. They didn't get all of the hotel amenities, but they had a clean, dry, and safe place to sleep. Have you experienced a "Jesus moment"—receiving kindness and compassion from someone just when you needed it? How has that encouraged you to be a giver of good and kind gestures yourself? As you go through the day, look for ways you can provide a "Jesus moment" to the people you encounter at work, at the grocery store, or in your home!

17 A REBELLIOUS SHEEP

Following the Shepherd

"I don't know why you won't eat what I make. You always loved my chicken casserole before. And I made your favorite dessert for lunch—rhubarb pie!"

I heard the manipulative whine in my mother's voice and responded coldly. "No thanks, Mom. I'll eat later."

"I don't think you've eaten in days. You'll feel better if you eat something," she pressed.

"I said no, Mom. I feel fine. I'm going out for a run."

I sprinted up the street, worried that the little dish of gelatin I had eaten the day before would add a pound.

Keep running. Burn it off.

I turned a corner and saw myself in a store window. My scale said I weighed just 98 pounds, but my eyes only saw the flab of an overweight creature who hid in her room all day and choked down food only when the hunger was overwhelming. A meal was that little dish of gelatin or 15 raisins or two spoonfuls of nonfat powdered milk—eaten dry.

As I sped up the street, I saw an old friend and cringed. I couldn't let her see me like this. I hurried out of sight up a side street and headed home for a round of jumping jacks and sit-ups.

I knew nothing about the term *anorexia nervosa* at that time, but for months I'd battled the terror that I might gain even a pound. I ruthlessly criticized my body, measuring my weight loss progress each day based on whether my thighs touched or if my fingers could circle my upper arm. Because of malnutrition my hair was thin and stringy and my clothes hung on me like a tablecloth. But I saw only fat.

Food was my enemy, and people tempted me to eat, so I spent most of my time alone. Obsessed with my diet and my exercise schedule, I had little use for friends or family even though I was desperately lonely.

All this time I also practiced another kind of discipline. For me, spiritual discipline meant Bible studies, church services, and strict control over my body, including weekly fasts from my already-minimal diet. I did grow spiritually during this time despite my distorted self-perception. Although I was no example of the joyful Christian, I certainly had the idea of discipline down pat—or that's what I thought.

Because of malnutrition my hair was thin and stringy and my clothes hung on me like a tablecloth.

When Philip Keller's *A Shepherd Looks at Psalm 23* was part of one of my Bible studies, I connected immediately with what I read in the book. Sheep, I discovered, are often afraid, confused, disoriented, and suspicious. Their unsettled nature leads them to ignore or even disobey their shepherd's guidance. I often felt like a rebellious sheep, seldom content but often frightened, disoriented, and suspicious. Sometimes I couldn't even get myself out of bed in the morning because I was a perfectionist and felt overwhelmed by expectations I felt that I and others had for my day.

Because I saw so many parallels between myself and sheep, Psalm 23 quickly became a favorite source of comfort and direction.

My sleep was usually filled with worries and fears, but one night I was awakened from a rare deep sleep by what seemed like a call. Immediately I thought of Psalm 23:5: "You prepare a feast for me in the presence of my enemies" (NLT). I imagined the scene—sheep grazing calmly in the open while the shepherd keenly watched to make certain no predator approached. What a peaceful image I had in my head of the shepherd's watchful care and the tranquil hearts of his sheep. *How nice,* I thought.

But God had a more difficult message for me. That night he began to teach me that my refusal to eat was a rebellion against his will and harmful to the body he had blessed me with. Food was *not* an enemy but a gift for me to enjoy without fear or doubt. In the dark of that night, God showed me that I was ignoring his leading and missing the tranquil pastures I pictured with Psalm 23. Like a rebellious sheep, I was wandering away on my own, going places where he was not leading. No wonder I found barren ground, fear, and real, physical danger.

"OK, Lord, I get it. You want me to eat. But I'm terrified. If I eat I'll get fatter. I'll go completely out of control and I want to be thin. I'm sorry that I haven't been listening. I'm sorry that I've botched my life so badly. I can't do this by myself. I can't eat and be OK about it. Please help me."

I immediately felt peace. I realized God cared enough to call me to stop hurting myself. Somehow I knew that if I did not listen and act, I would experience only more isolation and loneliness.

So I decided I would eat at regular mealtimes every day. I would force myself to eat in public with other people whenever possible. I would eat whatever was offered, starting with small portions. And I would be thankful.

I believe God's call that night saved my life.

My anorexia did not end immediately. Many months passed before I understood that eating is a normal and healthy behavior—not just for everyone else but for me too. But I turned a corner that night. I let the Good Shepherd carry me on his shoulders back to the flock, back to a peaceful place within his sight.

—Gloria Spielman

WHEN GOD BREAKS THROUGH

Sometimes we can see clearly in one area of life and yet be completely blind to sin and rebellion in another. Jesus died not just for the sins we commit against other people or the sins others perpetrate against us, but also for the sins we commit against ourselves. He is the Good Shepherd. He cares for us and wants us to be whole. He can give us that gift of wholeness only if we will trust him and follow his path.

MY CHALLENGE

Reflect on the following verses from Psalm 23: "You prepare a table before me in the presence of my enemies. You anoint my head with oil; my cup overflows. Surely goodness and love will follow me all the days of my life, and I will dwell in the house of the Lord forever" (Psalm 23:5–6, NIV). What do you need most from the Good Shepherd today? Pledge yourself to be his sheep—an obedient follower who willingly lets the Shepherd lead you to the perfect places and in the right ways.

18 PRACTICE DOESN'T MAKE PERFECT

Finding Perfection in Jesus

Kirstin is passionate about music. But still some practice sessions feel like a roller-coaster experience, and as her piano teacher/mother sitting next to her, I get a free ride.

So far this practice session had gone well. After playing her two favorite pieces mistake-free, five-year-old Kirstin gave me a big hug. Life was good.

"I'm going to play 'Musette' now," Kirstin declared. Her little fingers plinked out the music with the command of an accomplished musician. But then she blundered some notes. Her hands dropped to her lap. Our roller coaster car had stalled at the peak.

She glanced at me and began playing from the beginning again. When she stumbled over the same measure as before, the steep drop began.

Attempting to stop the free fall I suggested, "Try playing middle C with your third finger."

"I know. Please don't tell me." Kirstin's lower lip quivered. Her set face told me she would work out the issue on her own.

Kirstin has always been determined. Born two years after her brother, Joel, she tried to match him in every skill—running, swimming, reading, Bible memory, soccer, math, games, and of course, playing the piano. She had taught herself to play by listening to Joel practice. She didn't need me to tell her what she was doing wrong in "Musette."

Again she played from the beginning, but blundered the same notes. "I'll never be able to play this piece!" she wailed. She walked to the window pouting, tears in her eyes.

"You know that you have a gift for music," I tried to encourage her.

Kirstin lifted the piano lid and pretended to check the hammers inside.

I closed the lid. "Why don't you try 'Musette' just one more time?"

Still stalling, she tried to somersault over the piano bench.

Frustrated, I finally said, "You just have to keep practicing. Remember, practice makes perfect!"

Kirstin stopped fidgeting, sat back on the bench, played the piece, 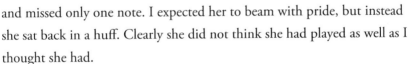 and missed only one note. I expected her to beam with pride, but instead she sat back in a huff. Clearly she did not think she had played as well as I thought she had.

"What is wrong? You did a great job! I loved how you played quieter and then louder, and you slowed down nicely at the end."

Sticking out her lower lip, she cried, "It wasn't perfect. I'll never be perfect!"

Stunned at the depth of her comment, I just sat there looking at her. She was right. She would never be perfect, and neither would I. *No matter how hard I try, I will never be perfect. No matter how hard I practice being content, patient, or worry free, these virtues still escape me. It's only a matter of time before I'm turning green with envy, shrouded in impatience, or gripped with worry. Practice doesn't make perfect.*

I took a deep breath, looked in my daughter's eyes, and said, "Oh, honey, no one but God is perfect! I know you can't be perfect, and God knows it too. When we ask him, Jesus washes away our sins. Then God sees us as perfect, but it's not something we can do on our own."

Sticking out her lower lip, she cried, "It wasn't perfect. I'll never be perfect!"

Kirstin looked straight at me. I said, "I don't expect you to be perfect, but you can keep practicing this song and try to make it as perfect as you can."

"I don't have to be perfect?"

I gave her a hug and said, "No, you don't. Want to try the piece again?"

Kirstin smiled, turned to the piano, and played "Musette."

—*Christine Erickson*

WHEN GOD BREAKS THROUGH

Maybe you have seen the bumper sticker that reads *Christians aren't perfect, just forgiven.* We will never reach perfection this side of heaven. Only one person has ever lived a sinless, perfect life: Jesus. Thankfully because of his sacrifice on the cross where he took on our sins, we are now considered perfect in God's eyes because "God made him who had no sin to be sin for us, so that in him we might become the righteousness of God" (2 Corinthians 5:21, NIV). We become perfect with God only through faith in his Son.

Yet that does not leave us off the hook to do whatever we want. We should continue to grow in our faith so that we might become more and more like Christ. As Paul encouraged the Ephesians, "Instead, we will hold to the truth in love, becoming more and more in every way like Christ, who is the head of his body, the church" (Ephesians 4:15, NLT). We may never be perfect on this earth, but we can practice!

MY CHALLENGE

On a scale of 1 to 10, with 1 being the least and 10 being the greatest, rate how much of a perfectionist you are. In what areas of your life are you driven to perfection? How does knowing the truth of 2 Corinthians 5:21 help you deal with this desire? Take a moment to thank God for sending Jesus to be perfect for you.

19 FREED TO FORGIVE
Finding Real Healing in Forgiveness

"Good evening, ma'am," the man on my side said, slickly. He set down the Styrofoam cooler he was carrying and smiled. One gold tooth glinted in the glow of the streetlight.

Before I could reply, he pushed me back into the car. "Give me all your money!" he demanded, smile gone.

I'd just arrived in Texas for graduate school from my home in New England. My fiancé, Rob, had made the drive with me, and then helped me unload and unpack all of my boxes in the apartment I'd share with several roommates. Rob and I had worked up an appetite and, job accomplished, we were ready for some burgers!

We dashed to the fast-food restaurant down the street and returned to the apartment complex. When we punched in my code and drove through the gate, we barely noticed the two young men who wandered into the parking lot behind my car.

The parking spots near the front of my building were filled, so Rob parked in the back. Just as we opened the car doors, the two men walked out of the shadows and met us, one on each side of the car.

The other man had pushed Rob back in the driver's seat, a gun pressed to his waist. "Give me all your money!" he demanded in a husky voice.

"We're students," Rob said, fear edging his voice.

"We don't have any money!" I pleaded.

"Where's your wallet? Give me all your money or I'll kill you!"

Rob had earlier tossed his wallet and cell phone onto the trunk of the car.

The men grabbed their loot. "Stay in the car!" They slammed the doors and ran off, their laughter lingering in the night air. Thankfully, we were not bodily harmed. We were safe.

Or were we? It is easy to say that God protected us that night, and he did. Still I struggled to sense God's presence in the days, months, and years after that night. Where was he when I woke with nightmares? When would I feel safe again?

Then a trusted friend suggested, "You won't heal until you forgive those men." I began to recognize the anger I still carried in my heart, and I knew I had to let it go. I began recording my feelings in a journal and started seeing a counselor for support, wisdom, and guidance.

"Give me all your money!" he demanded in a husky voice.

Freeing myself to forgive didn't take away my nightmares or immediately restore my sense of security, but it was a healthy step. Like a wound that needs cleaning before it can mend properly, my life needed a washing of forgiveness before I could move on and start to heal. Even with God's help, forgiving the men who had robbed us and violated my sense of safety was one of the hardest processes I've ever undergone.

Today I wear a scar. Sometimes you can see it in my apprehension in a parking lot. Sometimes it shows when I have to walk alone to my car at night. But beneath my scar lies a healed spirit because I no longer harbor anger or hatred for those men and I know that with time, even scars can fade.

—*Clarissa Moll*

WHEN GOD BREAKS THROUGH

When we have been wronged, forgiving the perpetrators is difficult. But the longer we hold on to bitterness, anger, and resentment, the more we hurt ourselves. Only when we forgive can we begin to heal emotionally and spiritually. Jesus commands us to forgive those who hurt us: "And when you stand praying, if you hold anything against anyone, forgive him, so that your Father in heaven may forgive you your sins" (Mark 11:25, NIV).

Paul reminds us that the key to such forgiveness is to "Bear with each other and forgive whatever grievances you may have against one another. Forgive as the Lord forgave you" (Colossians 3:13, NIV). When we truly understand God's infinite love and forgiveness for us, we will be able to offer that same forgiveness to others.

MY CHALLENGE

Whom do you need to forgive? Whom do you need to ask for forgiveness? Spend a few moments in prayer, and ask God to help you begin to forgive.

20 "What's Your Friend's Name?"

Knowing the Power of Jesus' Name

A rash of burglaries plagued our small, peaceful Texas neighborhood. People were frightened. Crime had seldom troubled our tranquil streets.

The police reported that the burglary suspect drove an older blue van and was breaking into homes during the day when most residents were at work, stealing everything from electronics and jewelry to tools and guns. They speculated that the criminal was possibly armed and dangerous.

During the time of this crime spree, my wife, Cherie, and I prayed daily for her protection because she was at home during the day while I was at work. Cherie was seven months pregnant with our Goliath-size son and looked as if she was preparing to deliver a washing machine.

My normally quiet wife bolted out our front door and halfway across our lawn to confront the man.

I called home several times a day to make sure Cherie was OK. However, my fears were unfounded. Cherie was not simply at home; she was on patrol. And the criminal picked the wrong woman to mess with.

One Thursday afternoon Cherie was reading mail at our dining room table near the bay window overlooking our front lawn. Our friends Jim and

Michelle lived across the street, and both of them were at work. For some reason Cherie looked up at just the right moment and saw a rusty, old blue van with tinted windows driving slowly down our street. The van passed Jim and Michelle's house, stopped, backed up, and parked at their curb. Cherie's internal radar buzzed off the charts.

The van sat there for several minutes, and no one got out. But Cherie kept watching. A hulking, bearded man in cutoff overalls got out and walked to Jim and Michelle's front door. He knocked, waited, and then rang the doorbell and waited some more. When no one answered he went to the carport and started going through  the storage cabinets. After a few moments he headed back to his truck with Jim's new chainsaw.

Cherie launched into action. Filled with fear and indignation, the boldness of faith, and a healthy dose of vigilante-mama-bear-protective instinct, my normally quiet wife bolted out our front door and halfway across our lawn to confront the man.

The man opened the sliding side door of his van, threw in the chainsaw and headed again toward the side door of the house.

"May I help you?" bellowed my very pregnant wife. The man looked up and saw the least intimidating person he had ever met. "Um, I'm just borrowing my friend's chainsaw," he answered.

"Oh, yeah?" Cherie shouted back. "What's your friend's name?"

"Uh, Mike," he stammered.

"Well, you got the wrong house then! You'd better put that chainsaw back right now!" Cherie ordered.

And he did! Then he ran down the driveway, hopped in his van, and sped off. Cherie returned to our house and called the police, who picked up the criminal minutes later with a van full of stolen items.

Cherie could have done nothing physically to stop this man from stealing from our friend. But the attempted crime was foiled because Cherie knew our friend's name—Jim. And no one was going to take his belongings without knowing that name, as long as Cherie was concerned.

That night, still stunned by everything that took place, Cherie and I held each other and thanked God for her safety. Now whenever I face a threat of any kind, I think of Cherie bellowing, "What's your friend's name?"

But unlike the burglar, I know the right answer: Jesus. And that makes all the difference in the world.

—Tom Burggraf

WHEN GOD BREAKS THROUGH

There is a thief on the prowl who is the enemy of our souls: the devil. The evil one will indeed knock at our door to try to steal, kill, and destroy (John 10:10, NIV). He loves to steal our faith, joy, hope, love, or anything else that's ours through the blessings of God. But when the thief does come, we know our friend's name: Jesus. And Jesus is even more protective of his friends than Cherie is of hers. Jesus assures us, "I am the good shepherd; I know my sheep and my sheep know me—just as the Father knows me and I know the Father—and I lay down my life for the sheep" (John 10:14–15). We can have confidence that our Good Shepherd is not merely hired to do a job, but is committed to caring for us—so much so that he willingly laid down his life for us. What better friend do you need in times of trouble, despair, or uncertainty?

MY CHALLENGE

The Gospel of John reveals many names Jesus used to refer to himself, pointing to the special roles he was to fulfill. For example, Jesus called himself the "bread of life" (6:35, NIV), "light of the world" (8:12), the "resurrection and the life" (11:25), "the way, the truth, and the life" (14:6), and the "true vine" (15:1). Which of Jesus' names means the most to you today? How does knowing his name help you in your situation?

21 SOMETHING CHANGED

Experiencing the Power of God's Transforming Love

I surveyed Gordon from my seat at my friend's wedding reception. Years before, Gordon and I had traveled Europe with a youth choir, belted out song after song in our high school musicals, and annoyed our English teacher with continual comments from the back of the room.

I had been out of high school for more than 10 years. All around me at the reception, like me, my former classmates sported thicker waistlines and thicker eyeglasses and some obviously had thicker wallets. But for Gordon, sitting next to me, even more had changed. A few years earlier Gordon had been crushed under an Army tank. That accident had taken his sight, his mobility, and much of his ability to communicate.

Gordon began to speak, and as I leaned closer to understand him, another classmate at the reception quietly pushed back her chair from our table. Sarah Mulroney had never had much patience with people who required extra effort. A conversation with Gordon required the extra measure Sarah wasn't willing to give. She tiptoed in a wide circle to avoid contact with her former friend and his wheelchair. "He can't see me anyway," she mouthed to the rest of us and walked toward the buffet.

Gordon couldn't see, but he had no trouble hearing. "Ba-dah did . . . ba-dah did . . . ba-dah did?"

I cupped my ear and concentrated as I tried to hear him. "Yeah, Gord?"

"B-dah did s-s-someone g-g-go?"

No question, I thought on my way home from the reception, Gordon was quite different from the guy we remembered singing in All-State Chorus and swimming the breaststroke on the swim team.

Over the next few years, my husband, David, and I enjoyed many visits with Gordon. We marveled at his tenacity and physical improvement as he learned to type by touch, speak more clearly, and walk with a cane, even though he had no feeling in his left leg.

When our 20-year class reunion arrived, David and I planned to spend time with Gordon and his wife, Sandy. We saw them at a corner table as soon as we walked into the reception hall and joined them for an evening of eating, laughing, and listening to music. Later, as I toured the dining room, I ran into Jim, who'd been my classmate and childhood neighbor.

Sometime in junior high Jim had become too cool for people like me. He was always in on the private jokes, every hair in place. Jim spent weekends with the crowd on the more exclusive Maple Lane. For one of our previous reunions, he swept in from Hawaii wearing a bright muscle shirt and a deep tan with a gorgeous woman on his arm. Jim hung out with the winners.

He stopped me and motioned in the direction of our table. "What happened?" he asked, pointing to Gordon with concern.

Soldiers heard Gordon's muffled screams and desperately dug through the desert sand until they found him

As I answered Jim's question, I realized he had never heard Gordon's story: how Gordon opened his tank's hatch cover during a nighttime training exercise; how the sand gave way and Gordon was thrown into the path of the tumbling machine; how soldiers heard Gordon's muffled screams and desperately dug through the desert sand until they found him and pulled him to safety.

When I finished speaking, Jim surprised me by going to our table and sitting next to Gordon.

"Gord, it's Jim," he said, touching Gordon on the arm. "Jim DeJulio. Remember?"

For the next hour Jim helped Gordon remember life as a kid in our small town. Together they sang the opening song from *Guys and Dolls*. Then two other guys who'd been on the swim team joined us. Gordon threw out joke after joke, entertaining our table and people beyond it. He listened as the guys described their families, jobs, and the places they lived. When the DJ began a favorite song, Gordon tapped Sandy and motioned toward the dance floor. Sandy handed Gordon his cane, and when the couple stood to dance, Jim led the crowd in an ovation that lasted until the song ended.

The next week I was looking through my reunion photographs when David walked in and peered over my shoulder.

"Let me see that one again." He reached for the pile of photos and pulled out one of Jim talking with Gordon. He looked at it closely and then pointed to something peeking out from under Jim's shirt cuff.

"A WWJD bracelet?" I asked. *What Would Jesus Do?* It was unmistakable, but I hadn't seen it that night.

Sandy's letter arrived a few days later. *After the reunion,* she wrote, *Gord commented that he hadn't remembered that the guys in your class were so nice.*

I smiled. Gordon didn't have a faulty memory. Something changed. For Jim, at least, it wasn't just the mellowing of age, I suspected. I assumed that he had clearly responded to the Holy Spirit's call. He was being transformed into the likeness of the man whose name he wore on his wrist. I pray that kind of change is happening in my life too.

—*Martha Manikas-Foster*

WHEN GOD BREAKS THROUGH

The apostle Paul wrote of the transformation that comes when we meet and follow the Savior: "We, who with unveiled faces, all reflect the Lord's glory, are being transformed into his likeness with ever-increasing glory, which comes from the Lord, who is the Spirit" (2 Corinthians 3:18, NIV). Transformation is more than a desire to be a better person. It means you're taking steps in that direction. The first step is faith in Christ. Becoming Christlike, however, is not instantaneous. As Paul mentioned, we "*are being* transformed." The process is ongoing.

MY CHALLENGE

What does the process of transformation look like in your life? Make a mental map of your life for the past few years. What changes have others noticed about you? Ask your spouse, another family member, or a friend to give you feedback on the ways he or she sees God transforming you.

22 JAILHOUSE FAITH
Seeking God Wherever We Are

"Why do you spend so much time in Bible study?" my son asked.

His question stunned me. He was right—I did spend a lot of time leading two different Bible studies at church.

As we talked I learned his words were motivated by more than simply concern about the time I spent. He was concerned about *whom* I was leading the studies for—or more correctly—whom I *wasn't*.

My son had been arrested for DUI charges and had just spent 10 days in jail. While there he had witnessed to men who were lost, desperate, and despondent. He had seen men who hungered for help and who needed to hear God's Word. So he wondered why I taught people in churches who already knew Jesus and God's Word. Why didn't I reach people like those men who cried out for help?

I had never considered that.

But as I did, the thought of entering a jail shook me. What did I have to offer people who had been judged guilty of some crime? How could I possibly identify with them? As I continued to contemplate and pray about this, I decided to take my son's challenge seriously and joined a women's jail ministry.

Riding the elevator to the fourth floor of the jail on my first visit, I prayed that I would be able to love the women unconditionally. Once in the room preparing to start the study, I watched nervously as women in orange-and-white-stripe uniforms filed off the elevator and into the room where chapel was held. What a variety of ages, races, sizes, and shapes!

My eyes and heart searched each face. Some women would not look at me. Some smiled and greeted me. Some shook my hand. Others accepted a hug. I was surprised to realize that these women were created by God, just as I was, and they needed his grace and mercy, just as I did.

And I found other surprises in jail. I found compassion. We began our time together with prayer, and the requests poured in for parents, children, and husbands. The women were also concerned about each other. They prayed for the other women in their cell blocks and for the conflicts they experienced with others. They prayed for upcoming trials, but most often they prayed that when they left jail, they would not return.

My eyes were also opened to the battles these women faced. One woman confessed her need to give up the harmful relationships with men she too often pursued. She had ended up back in prison because of her need for a man's love and approval. Another sister in Christ confided that she was glad to be in jail because she felt God had put her there so she could change her life.

I found hope. Some women attended chapel and Bible study, seeking a relationship with Jesus that could help them stand firm and battle their addictions. As I got to know the women, I watched them grow spiritually. One woman told us about a box she filled with Scripture verses on pieces of paper. When others came to her with problems and perplexities, they would draw a Bible verse out of the box, and the message amazingly always fit the situation. These sisters were discovering God's power to speak to those who seek him.

I found renewal. One woman in her thirties told of the changes in her life that resulted from listening to God during the several months she was incarcerated before her hearing. She had been released for a week to await disposition of her case. During that week she treasured the opportunities to care for her children, walk in the rain, watch the moon rise, go to church, and even mop her kitchen floor! She was discovering the joys of surrendering her battle to the Lord, standing firm on the truths she had learned in Bible study here at the jail, and going forward with God at her right hand.

What did I have to offer people who had been judged guilty of some crime? How could I possibly identify with them?

Today, I am thankful my son sent me to jail! When I tell people I am going to jail, I smile because of what I have found there and because I am learning that the Lord speaks to us when we seek him—no matter where we are.

—Barbara Collier

ALONG THE WAY

WHEN GOD BREAKS THROUGH

God very clearly explains that to know him and have a relationship with him, we must earnestly seek him. The path to knowing God is not easy. The seeker must make an effort and be persistent. But the rewards are great. As we persistently pursue God, we will find him. As the Proverbs writer states, "I love those who love me, and those who seek me find me" (Proverbs 8:17, NIV). It doesn't matter where we are, who we are, or what our circumstances in life may be. God extends the invitation to everyone: "Seek me and you will find me."

MY CHALLENGE

Look up these verses: Deuteronomy 4:29; 1 Chronicles 28:9; Psalm 145:18; Jeremiah 29:13; and Lamentations 3:25. Choose one to memorize. Consider your own relationship with God. What steps can you take to know God better?

No Agenda

Influencing Others With Christ's Love

We lived in Portland, Oregon, for years. But not until we were moving did we realize how little we had invested in our neighborhood. As a result, with new opportunities before us, we began praying that God would lead us exactly where he wanted us in establishing a new home and new friends.

When we arrived in our new neighborhood in Wellington, New Zealand, we realized that it is actually quite hard in suburbia to know your neighbors. Even the architecture lends itself to privacy and individuality. We have gone from front porches to back decks, scattered toys on the lawn to six-foot fences, and open front doors to entering our homes through automatic garage door openers.

When Julie and Tom and their daughter, Theresa, moved next door soon after our arrival, we welcomed them, but they seemed quite content to keep us at a distance—the over-the-fence type of neighbors. My wife and I decided simply to be authentic. In one conversation, though we chose our words carefully, we revealed that we followed Jesus. After an awkward moment the conversation ended, and then the "fences" grew taller.

We kept at our efforts with some small initiatives. First we brought our neighbors' "wheely bin" (a wheeled garbage can) in from the street each week. Our houses were off the street, down a shared drive. We never said a word, just put it at their garage door. Then the delivery guy asked if we would sign for some packages for them. We readily agreed.

After our kids became friends with Theresa, we began praying with our kids for our neighbors. When school break came, we knew Tom and Julie needed child care. We offered to let Theresa stay with us, and they took us up on it.

That first week my wife made dinner for both families, not knowing if they would accept our last-minute offer to join us for a meal. When they came to collect their daughter after a tiring day at work, they readily agreed to stay.

A couple of months later, we were shocked when they asked us to take a short vacation with them. We were not really ready to go on a trip but said yes because we valued the friendship. This time bonded us more deeply.

During that trip Julie and Tom told us they were not doing well as a couple. They split up a few months later, and we were saddened by their ugly divorce. But during this difficult process, we saw the greatest advance in our friendship. Theresa needed the stability of our family. Julie and Theresa often joined us for meals and outings, and Theresa stayed with us during each school break. We even coordinated swim lessons, gymnastics, and other routine schedules to include her.

Over the next year we came to know Julie's story. She had brief but ugly experiences with people who called themselves Christians.

At Christmas we knew Julie and Theresa would be alone, and we wanted to include them in our holiday events. My wife asked them to join us to celebrate a family tradition of having a birthday cake for Jesus. It was the first year of that tradition, but we didn't reveal that fact.

After the gifts and cake, I read a children's Christmas story, and our kids played while we chatted. We didn't try to convince them of the Christian message. We let them gain the facts over time.

Over the next year we came to know Julie's story. She had brief but ugly experiences with people who called themselves Christians. I don't know if they knew they communicated such negative images to her, but it made us very aware of how nonbelievers might perceive us.

Meanwhile, Julie often came over for a cup of tea with my wife who would engage in the spiritual act of boiling the kettle and listening. Sometimes she'd seize the moment to speak truth that comforted.

I remember Julie's asking, "Why is God letting this happen to us?" My wife gently took her hand and told her that God did not do this—her ex-husband did—and that God loved her unconditionally. The tears really poured then.

When Christmas came around during the next two years, Julie asked our advice about which Bibles they might buy. The following year she asked if they might go to a Christmas service with us. Now—after three years of friendship—we openly spoke of spiritual things.

None of my family remembers when Julie and her daughter became believers. Mom and daughter now pray together daily, read their Bibles, and discuss how much they trust and love Jesus. We laugh as Julie speaks boldly to her friends about Jesus—much more boldly than she would ever have tolerated.

We moved this year. One of the hardest parts was leaving Julie and Theresa. We hear from them regularly, and they are coming to see us in a couple of months. They are even talking about moving near us.

As we prepared to move this time, we eagerly prayed for the neighborhood and people we'd meet there and for the next adventure they would bring to us.

—*Mike Brantley*

WHEN GOD BREAKS THROUGH

We usually know when someone has an agenda. We recognize the gleam in the eye, followed by, as Mike put it, "the hard sell." Books on how to influence others proclaim that this is the way to "hook" someone. If there is no "sale," you cut bait and move on. But many people have been hurt by this technique. Perhaps you're one of them—someone who was simply "another soul" for the kingdom for somebody seeking quantity rather than quality.

Jesus proposed a "radical" solution for influencing others.

> "Jesus replied, 'You must love the LORD your God with all your heart, all your soul, and all your mind.' This is the first and greatest commandment. A second is equally important: 'Love your neighbor as yourself.' The entire law and all the demands of the prophets are based on these two commandments"(Matthew 22:37–40, NLT).

Loving others may sound simplistic, but it can be the toughest "non-agenda" action you will ever perform.

MY CHALLENGE

What practical things can you do to show love to those around you? Do you know someone who has resisted your kindness in the past or who views even a tiny act of love as "part of an agenda"? Pray for him or her, asking God to help you meet a need he or she might have.

24 The Sleep of the Innocent

Resting in the Father's Constant Care

Several years ago we spent Thanksgiving week in Kansas with my mother and two older brothers. The time with my family went by pretty quickly, and next thing I knew we were driving to the Kansas City airport to head back to warm, sunny Miami, Florida. If you have ever tried to get a family of five from point A to point B—especially when points A and B are 1,250 miles and two sold-out airplanes apart—you can appreciate the effort involved. The expression "herding cats" comes to mind.

Because it was a holiday, the flights were all packed—not an empty seat anywhere. The airline resorted to bribery to try to free up a couple of seats. We turned down two free round-trip tickets accompanied by a hundred dollars apiece. We didn't want to give up our seats.

Of course all of this caused our flights to run late. Many people around us in the airports and on the planes were concerned about making their connections and what they would do if they missed them. My fifteen-month-old daughter, Savannah, had no such worries about connections. Somewhere over the Midwest, she decided to sit with me awhile. After inspecting everything in my shirt pocket at least a dozen times, Savannah yawned, stretched, and fell sound asleep in my lap. The only connection she was concerned about was the one with me and my lap—and that was right on time, right where it was supposed to be.

During our flight we ran through several patches of turbulence—enough to make people click their seatbelts on and reach for their drinks. At least once we experienced one of those drops that evokes a lot of "Ohhhhs" from passengers and reassuring words from the pilot. Again Savannah slept through it all. No white knuckles on those little hands. She kept sleeping soundly.

Finally we landed in Miami, a little late and a little frazzled but together and glad to be home. Savannah didn't flinch when we bounced on the tarmac. She didn't clench the armrest when the plane braked hard. She didn't try to be the first one in the aisle when we stopped. In fact she never even stirred

During our flight we ran through several patches of turbulence— enough to make people click their seatbelts on . . .

until I took off my seatbelt and stood up with her to leave the plane. Then she opened those baby blues, rubbed her eyes and face and smiled. "Daddy!" she said, as though she were surprised to see me there in Miami.

My baby daughter was not concerned about getting from point A to point B (or C or D or E). All she needed was a warm lap and her daddy's arms surrounding her, keeping her safe and secure.

Isn't that what we all need on our journey of life?

—*Kent Keller*

When God Breaks Through

Do not be anxious about anything, but in everything, by prayer and petition, with thanksgiving, present your requests to God. And the peace of God, which transcends all understanding, will guard your hearts and your minds in Christ Jesus (Philippians 4:6–7, NIV).

God's Word says we can have peace that passes understanding when the turbulence comes—and it always comes. Content in our Father's arms, we can be satisfied with the arrangements and the circumstances God has ordained for us right now and not be consumed with the next connection, meeting, appointment, paycheck, whatever. Isn't that what Jesus meant when he said, "Therefore do not worry about tomorrow, for tomorrow will worry about itself. Each day has enough trouble of its own" (Matthew 6:34, NIV).

If we can learn to rest in God's presence as a child rests in her father's arms, then the day will come that we arrive home, rub the sleep from our eyes, and cry, "Abba! Father!"

My Challenge

Write down Philippians 4:6–7 on an index card—or several of them. Post the cards where you can easily see them—at the kitchen sink, at your desk, on the dashboard of your car. When you feel anxieties start to creep into your mind, read these verses. Then offer your worries to God, trusting that he will fill your heart and mind with his peace.

25 DISMISSED!

Finding Forgiveness in an Unexpected Place

"Oh, no!" My adrenaline surged when I saw the red and blue lights in the rearview mirror. I checked the speedometer. Ten miles over the speed limit.

"Oh, no!" I groaned again, pulling into a parking lot.

"What's wrong, Mommy?" asked Lauren, my four-year-old daughter. "Is everything OK?"

"Everything's fine," I said, as much to reassure myself as her. In his car seat, my infant son whimpered as if in sympathy.

With shaking hands, I lowered the window, opened the glove compartment, and pulled out the registration and insurance papers. Handing them to a stone-faced police officer, I said, "I'm sorry, sir. I didn't realize how fast I was going. I'm on my way to a Bible study at my church." I patted the Bible lying on the passenger seat next to a box of cheese crackers, hoping my reference to God's Word might spark thoughts of grace and mercy.

"May I see your driver's license, ma'am?" the officer asked.

"Of course," I said, reaching for my purse and pulling out my quilted wallet. Then a sick feeling gripped me. I had put my credit card, lipstick, and driver's license in my black dress purse the day before when my family had gone out for lunch. That purse was still on my kitchen counter.

Horrified, I stared at the officer. "Oh, dear," I said. "I have a license. But it's in my other purse." Would the officer understand the importance of changing purses to match outfits?

Apparently he didn't.

"Ma'am, unfortunately driving without a license in the state of Ohio is a first-degree misdemeanor. You'll have to go to court next week and stand before a judge."

"But I'm a law-abiding citizen!" I wailed. "My last speeding ticket was in high school! I'm just a frazzled mom. It was an honest mistake."

"I'm sorry, ma'am. You'll be expected at the county courthouse one week from today."

"Is the police officer going to take you to jail, Mommy?" asked Lauren.

"No, no. Everything will be OK," I said. My words felt forced, and I knew she didn't believe me. "Let's just go home."

The rest of the week, I badgered myself with accusations. How could I have forgotten my license? How could I explain a first-degree misdemeanor on an otherwise spotless record? I was the wife of a U.S. Air Force chaplain. I was expected to maintain the highest degree of integrity, especially because my husband's career was upholding God and country—including the country's laws. My reputation could never be laundered once the charge was documented.

I rehearsed my speech to the judge at least a hundred times. After entering a plea of no contest, I would explain my mistake. I prayed God would give me a female judge who understood the importance of purse-and-outfit coordination.

My husband promised to meet me at the courthouse, but he called my cell phone just as I arrived there with Lauren and my son. He assured me he was on his way. So the children and I sat waiting for court to begin. My son let everyone know he was missing his nap while Lauren spilled raisins and tried to eat them off the floor.

"All rise," the bailiff announced.

The gray-haired judge strode to his bench. I couldn't believe I was counted among this roomful of people who were probably real criminals.

My husband still hadn't arrived when my name was called. I would have to deal with two squirming children in front of the judge. "Lauren," I said in my strictest, no-nonsense voice. "Sit here and be quiet."

Shaking, with my son wriggling in one arm and my driver's license in hand, I approached the bench.

The judge peered at me over his glasses. "I can see here that you showed proof of insurance."

"Yes, sir," I replied, trying to set up my prepared response in my mind.

The judge looked at my son who was pulling my hair and loudly protesting being held in my arms.

Horrified, I stared at the officer. "Oh, dear," I said. "I have a license. But it's in my other purse."

"That's *my* mommy," I heard Lauren announce proudly to the people near her, followed by a few chuckles.

"I can see you're a busy young mom," the judge continued. "In the case of this citation, I'm going to dismiss the charge. Dismissed as groundless." *Bam!* His gavel emphasized his words.

Relief filled my heart as I mentally threw away my rehearsed speech. I needed no defense after all.

Gratitude flooded my heart. This wasn't a life-and-death pardon, but it was an unexpected and overwhelming reminder of God's grace and mercy.

With a thankful smile I plucked my daughter from her seat and hurried out of the courtroom. "You're lucky," a clerk remarked as I left. "He doesn't usually dismiss charges."

Perhaps he doesn't, I thought, *but I know a God who does.*

Back at the helm of my minivan, carefully watching the speedometer, I knew I hadn't been lucky. I had simply received God's grace and favor.

—*Heidi Spencer*

WHEN GOD BREAKS THROUGH

Think about the last time someone hurt you—whether intentionally or not. Maybe someone overlooked your contribution to an important task, or maybe you received one of those backhanded compliments that aren't really compliments. Most of us can come up with a list of wrongs that other people have committed against us. Sometimes those offenses fade with time. At other times they remain as fresh as if they had happened yesterday.

Reflect on this truth about God's forgiveness from Psalm 103:12: "As far as the east is from the west so far has he removed our transgressions from us" (NIV). East never, ever meets West. Never will. Never can. That's as far as God has removed our *daily* and moment-by-moment transgressions that we have committed against him. We need never wallow in the past; nor will we hear God bring up the bad name we called a friend in grade school or the neighbor we forgot to help out. Our record has been completely wiped clean because of what Jesus did on the cross for us. That act dismissed all charges. And we need to offer others that same type of forgiveness.

MY CHALLENGE

Do you struggle with guilt or shame over a particular event or circumstance of your life? Write down those self-condemning thoughts and then tear the paper into little pieces or burn it as a symbol of Christ's forgiveness in your life. Remember that Jesus' death on the cross brings pardon from the penalty of your sins, now and at the final judgment.

26 LOST AND FOUND
Putting a Face to God's Loving Care

"Somebody! Somebody!" The little boy's plaintive cry split the air of the bus station.

Only a moment before, I'd watched the child of about six or seven years ambling along without a care in the world, walking with a slight limp. As he'd come closer, I recognized the smile and pleasant, jovial countenance of a child with Down syndrome.

Then he'd reached the crowded bus stop, turned around, and looked back. Suddenly his engaging smile had turned upside down. Perplexity and fear crossed his face as he'd realized he was all alone.

I wondered if my face had reflected that same perplexity when my wife, Cindy, and I climbed off the bus and realized we weren't in Interlaken, Switzerland, where we'd looked forward to spending the day. As we sat in silent aggravation waiting for the *right* bus, I noticed how quiet the crowded bus station was.

During our few months in Rüschlikon, a suburb of Zurich, we had found the Swiss to be polite but not overly friendly when they were away from their homes. They rarely spoke to one another in public places, much less to American tourists.

"Somebody! *Somebody!*" His piercing cry in English became louder and tears streamed down his face. The crowd parted as people distanced themselves from this bewildered child.

"Somebody! Somebody!" he shouted all the louder, his face growing white with fright.

Somebody should do something, I thought, and started to move. But I wasn't fast enough. Suddenly a thirty-something young woman appeared with dark hair cascading down on a black raincoat. With a German accent and in broken English, she said ever so softly, "Somebody, somebody."

She hugged the boy and he wrapped his arms around his neck "Everything will be OK," she comforted. "You don't have to worry. You don't have to cry."

Our bus arrived and we boarded. But as we waited for the bus to pull away from the curb, we saw another young woman run to the bus stop with panic on her face. She spotted the woman holding the little boy, dashed to them, and put her arm around the child. The boy looked up. Immediately he slid into her arms and hugged her. His tears subsided, and an innocent smile reemerged.

"Somebody! Somebody!" His piercing cry in English became louder and tears streamed down his face.

My wife and I realized at the same time that the second woman was apparently the boy's mother. The first woman was simply a kind person who had reached out in love to someone hurting and in need. Ignoring the unwritten law of disengagement governing the crowd around her, she had done the unexpected and stooped down to help a child.

The bus pulled away. My wife smiled at me. I took her hand and silently thanked God for watching over that little boy, and us, in Switzerland and every day.

—*Rick Ezell*

WHEN GOD BREAKS THROUGH

God looks for believers through whom to do his work. Dozens of people witnessed the lost little boy's tearful plight, but only one chose to step in. God has good deeds in mind for each of us to accomplish. Ephesians 2:10 tells us that God "created us anew in Christ Jesus, so that we can do the good things he planned for us long ago" (NLT). As Paul instructed the Galatians, we, too, need to look for every opportunity to do good to everyone, "Whenever we have the opportunity, we should do good to everyone, especially to our Christian brothers and sisters" (Galatians 6:10, NLT).

MY CHALLENGE

Who are the lost people in your life today? Who needs a kind word or the warm embrace of friendship? As you go through the day, ask God to open your eyes to opportunities to do good. Look for ways you can be the face of God's love and compassion.

I SURRENDER
Acknowledging God's Place in Our Lives

"Mommy, Mommy! Don't leave me!" my 19-month-old daughter cried clinging to me while her four-year-old brother hung on my leg. We were standing outside their father's house waiting for him to answer the door.

After the divorce had been finalized, the courts ruled that the children were to go back and forth between two houses on weekends. And each time the children had to leave me, their trauma seemed to worsen.

I had heard them cry before, but tonight was different. In that moment, as I turned to leave them with their father, the life that lay ahead for these two little ones became clear to me.

They would always live in the tension of two households—two ways of celebrating Christmas and Easter, two sets of rules for behavior, two sets of friends. They would not have a sweet, innocent childhood. Instead, they would walk a tightrope between their dad and me.

As my ex-husband opened the door just enough to pull our daughter out of my arms, my heart was torn with remorse. Up until that moment I considered myself to be a feminist. I thought I was a strong, capable woman, living outside the traditional norms of society. I had marched and picketed to win various freedoms. I had access to divorce, access to jobs—and now I had children in pain.

Their tears melted the icy independence I had worked so hard to achieve in my life. I didn't feel like a strong woman at that moment. Instead I felt like an inadequate mother—a mother who put her own needs ahead of those of her children.

As I headed toward the car I told myself, "My children deserve better." But those words didn't do much to relieve the hollow feeling in the pit of my stomach. With all my might I wanted to blame my ex and society, as though forces outside myself were responsible for this situation. But I knew better. That was just another arrogant pose, like many I had assumed over the years. This time I knew I would have to take responsibility for what was happening.

Throughout my marriage I had asserted myself as independent and self-righteous, tallying up equality as a 50/50 split of all responsibilities. That sense of justice and entitlement left no room for Paul's definition of love as "patient, kind . . . it keeps no record of wrongs" (1 Corinthians 13:4–5, NIV).

Waiting for me in the car was someone who wanted to show me a different way. My friend Jurgen shocked me by saying, "None of us are free. Not if we think freedom is having things our own way. The only freedom we have is inside us. We are free to ask God for help. Everything else is rebellion against the sovereignty of God."

Then he said something that made me see my life in a whole new way. "Either God is God, or man is God."

I decided to join him in surrendering to God. As we said a prayer for the children, I envisioned myself standing before God and humbly asking for his help. I decided at that moment to put my problems in God's strong and sure hands and stop struggling to do everything my way.

Later that evening I called to check on the children. My daughter was still crying in the background, and now their father agreed, "You can come and get them early."

My burden lifted right then. God had responded immediately to prayer. He was saying, "I am watching over the children."

Even though I had turned my back on God during those years of strong willfulness, God had never left me.

Then he said something that made me see my life in a whole new way. "Either God is God, or man is God."

Now he was showing me a different way. The responsibility for changing the world and righting the wrongs could be placed in his powerful hands, not my own inadequate ones. Equipped with this new awareness, I went to get the children. They slept peacefully in the car on the way home.

As I carried one child and then the other inside the house, I prayed that they would be able to withstand the chaos of divorce. I realized the strength they needed would come from God. My job was simply to point them to him.

And they wouldn't need any picket signs to win that great love.

—*Judith Costello*

WHEN GOD BREAKS THROUGH

Ever find yourself caught between two competing ways of life? Many of us are caught between wanting to live our lives our way—being totally in charge—and living according to God's way—acknowledging that *he's* in charge. The people of Israel during Old Testament times experienced a similar tug-of-war. But Joshua, the leader of the people of Israel after the death of Moses, challenged them to choose: "If serving the LORD seems undesirable to you, then choose for yourselves this day whom you will serve. . . . But as for me and my household, we will serve the LORD" (Joshua 24:15, NIV). There is no middle ground.

MY CHALLENGE

What is the tug-of-war of your life? Are you caught between two opportunities or competing ways of life? Or are you caught between wanting to run your life and allowing God to do so? Consider Joshua's challenge. How do your actions show which choice you made?

28 THE UNEXPECTED GIFT

Living in God's Love

Six a.m. comes too early any day, and an hour-and-fifteen-minute commute is always too long. But as this certain workday began, it seemed especially difficult.

I had promised and committed this time in the morning to daily prayer. As tempted as I was to listen to an audiobook or catch National Public Radio for the morning news, I resisted. I had given this time to God, and it had become special to me.

Talking to God in the solitude of my car brought insight to my heart and mind. My daily profession came from Psalm 118:24: "This is the day that the LORD has made; let us rejoice and be glad in it" (NIV). And my affirmation followed: "Lord, you have created this day, and you have created me. May your purposes be fulfilled in me this day."

But I longed for more. On this day I asked God to let me know that I was a *particular* element and not a *general* part in his design. I wanted to know that I was on God's mind. I wanted to see God do something in my life so powerful that I knew it came from him. That was my prayer that morning.

Of course, when I arrived at work, the busyness of the day pushed my mind beyond the prayer of the morning. Finally work was over, and I was ready to prepare for the evening. I smiled with anticipation—Jean had invited me over to her house for a cup of tea.

Jean was the friend my heart had yearned for. We had connected through a small study group at church that included people with kids and a few singles like me. Most of us scattered in different directions when our monthly meetings were over, but Jean and I always seemed to snatch some piece of time to connect before the meeting or over dessert at the end. We moved easily into talk beyond work or the weather to conversation of the heart.

And now Jean had invited me over to her house for a cup of tea after she put her children to bed. In Jean's kitchen, I selected a lemon-flavored tea from the assortment she offered. She poured hot water in my cup, and I  dunked my tea bag, letting it steep until the water began to color and the fragrance wafted. I spooned sugar into the cup, stirred, inhaled, and then sipped. It was just right, just as I hoped our conversation would be over the next hour.

But then Jean abruptly said, "I have something for you." She handed me a pink envelope and continued. "I don't know why, but I felt I needed to give this to you. God laid it on my heart to do this."

I looked at the envelope. "Should I open it now or wait until later?" I asked.

"You can do whatever you'd like," she said, smiling. "It's yours."

"Then I'll open it now, so I can thank you appropriately." I pulled open the handcrafted envelope and read the message on the page inside. It began, "It is hard to explain why you are getting this gift . . . "

I was distracted by a check that started to slide out of the envelope. A large check. I was puzzled. I couldn't imagine why Jean was giving this to me. For a moment I just held the check. Then I finished reading Jean's note: "Please receive this as a gesture of love from your Abba Father. He knows you and loves you."

"I don't know why, but I felt I needed to give this to you. God laid it on my heart to do this."

Now I understood why this gift had come. It was the answer to my prayer of the morning. I knew without a doubt that God had heard my prayers and that through my dear friend, he was showing me that I was special to him.

I could only say "thank you" to Jean, touched by the gesture and knowing that under any other circumstance, I couldn't have accepted such a gift.

Jean offered suggestions of fun things I could do with the check. A ticket to a play? Maybe apply it to a trip? But the gift was the impetus for me to join a group of people from my church for a short-term mission trip. Out of the blue, I had experienced the *particular* love and care of God through my friend. I wanted to share that special love with others.

—*Karen Young*

WHEN GOD BREAKS THROUGH

God is the source of all love. He loved us enough to send his Son, Jesus, as the perfect sacrifice for our sins. And he loves us enough to listen to our heartfelt yearnings. Once we have been touched by God's love—whether through an answer to prayer, the comfort of a friend, or the warm smile of a stranger—we cannot remain unmoved. Our hearts will be kindled, and we will spread that love to others. John, who is often called the "apostle of love," stated this truth: "Dear friends, let us continue to love one another, for love comes from God. Anyone who lives is born of God and knows God. But anyone who does not love does not know God—for God is love" (1 John 4:7–8, NLT).

MY CHALLENGE

Biblical love is not a feeling, but a choice and an action. Read through the words of 1 Corinthians 13:4–7. Consider how you have displayed that type of love to others. What choices or actions can you take to display that love to someone in your family, at work, or even a stranger you encounter today?

29 UNCHARTED TERRITORY

Navigating Life's Unexpected Turns

"Oh, please, Lord!" I begged as I pushed through the crowd to the bulletin board. Surely my name would be on the list this time! Certainly the Lord wouldn't give me such a strong desire to minister and not open the doors.

My eyes focused on the list where my name should be. It wasn't there. Again. I turned away from the board, trying to control the disappointment that gnawed at my heart—trying to control the surge of tears until I returned to my dorm room.

When I arrived on the campus of my Christian college, I was on fire. Like many 18-year-olds, I thought I had life figured out. During high school I had been to camps and outreach events that featured ministry teams from Christian colleges. As these role models shared their testimonies and talents, they impacted my life.

Now it was my turn. I'd mapped out my plan for my life, which included serving on a campus ministry team—along with hundreds of other students who also dreamed of being on these teams.

I wanted to serve in the musical ministries, positions only available by audition. Not only was competition stiff, but auditioning was also a new and frightening concept to me. However, keeping my plan in mind, I forged ahead.

Each time the lists of newly formed teams were hung in the student center, hopefuls like me mobbed the bulletin boards and nervously scanned the rosters to see if we made the cut. Some students squealed with excitement, included among the elite. But time after time I walked away rejected. First a choir, then a music ministry traveling team, then a camp ministry. I winced and shrank a little more into myself as each door closed. My dream of spending weekends and summers traveling to churches, schools, rallies, and camps as part of one of those ministries slowly withered.

So much for my itinerary. Life was definitely not what I had expected after all. I was hurt and angry. It wasn't fair. I had as much to give as *this* person. I was *at least* as talented as *that* person. I felt unjustly rejected.

Before long I learned that while being part of one of those groups might have been an exciting and rewarding experience, God had something more important for me to do.

So much for my itinerary. Life was definitely not what I had expected after all.

My mother had been diagnosed with cancer shortly before I started college. By my sophomore year she was deteriorating rapidly. My father spent all of his off-hours caring for her, taking her to doctors, and visiting her in the hospital. Because I did not have any commitments that required me to stay on campus during weekends, I went home every weekend during that spring term.

I did the laundry that Mom couldn't do and Dad didn't have time to do. I shopped for groceries and did other tasks that had become too burdensome for my parents. Most important, I got to spend time with Mom.

Mom died three weeks after school ended for the year. If I'd succeeded in one of my many musical auditions, I would have missed out on that spring with her. I wouldn't have had the privilege of caring for my mother's needs. I wouldn't have experienced the incredible blessing of watching her dignity, beauty, and grace in suffering. And I wouldn't have been there to pray with and assist my father over the next two months before he, too, passed away.

The rejection I had faced was nothing compared to the God-given blessing of that time with my parents.

Nearly 30 years have passed since those difficult days, and now rejection is changing my expected course again. Divorce and surviving as a single mom, especially after 24 years of marriage, were certainly not even considered as part of my life map. This time, however, while I don't understand why I am facing this new rejection, I know I'm not rejected by the One who matters most. What once might have destroyed me has instead become God's proving ground of his faithfulness in my life.

He has provided a home, employment, and transportation. He has fortified my relationships with my two married daughters and their husbands, mobilized our church family as a support team, and galvanized our extended family with unbreakable bonds. Through his Word, he has gently softened areas of my heart that I didn't even know were hard. He has given me rest and peace deep in my soul.

This new road I'm traveling is still under construction, so navigation is awkward and painful. I can't foresee every roadblock, nor do I know what exciting landmarks I'll encounter. But as I journey through uncharted territory again, I know I'm not alone.

—Sharon Wright

WHEN GOD BREAKS THROUGH

No matter how much we plan, prepare, and predict, life throws surprises at us. The unexpected—or unimaginable—occurs. A death. A divorce. A sudden moment that forever changes us.

"That wasn't part of the plan," we cry. As we make our plans, we need to hold them loosely. The road ahead is always uncharted territory, under construction. We look down that road and can't see far. We plan our route and then give the map to God, knowing that he sees to the end of our road. He knows just what we need today so we arrive where he wants us to be tomorrow. When we look back, we will discover that the road we traveled was all part of God's grand itinerary for us.

MY CHALLENGE

How would you draw a map of your life? Have you traveled through some pleasant valleys? Enjoyed some scenic views? Passed along treacherous trails? Found some glorious surprises along the way? Take a moment to actually draw a map (or a timeline) of your life in recent weeks, months, or years. Consider the path on which you've come and thank God for his guidance and presence. Then, as you look down the road into the future, pray with the psalmist, "Show me the path where I should walk, O LORD; point out the right road for me to follow. Lead me by your truth and teach me, for you are the God who saves me. All day long I put my hope in you" (Psalm 25:4–5, NLT).

30 COURTROOM DRAMA

Hearing From God Through His Word

I sat in the courtroom shaking uncontrollably. My friend Deena sat next to me and took my hand in an effort to calm my frazzled nerves. My husband put his arm around my shoulders. I had never been in a courtroom before, and I hoped I would never have to be in one again.

I had been called as a witness for the defense in a heated family dispute over an estate issue. I was expected to testify on behalf of the accused. For three hours I listened to the plaintiff's witnesses, unable to take notes because of my shaking hands. I finally put away my pen, deciding to rely on my husband's notes.

I had spent the day before with the defense attorney and all his witnesses reviewing pertinent information, the questions the attorney would ask, and the questions that arise in cross-examination. This exercise was meant to calm the fears of those who had never testified in court, but it had the opposite effect on me.

When I got home, my husband tried to comfort me. "Your testimony will be so helpful, honey. Hang in there. It will all be over tomorrow afternoon."

I could only think of courtroom scenes in movies and on TV, with angry people like Jack Nicholson shouting, "You can't handle the truth!"

As much as I wanted to help, my overwhelming desire was to run home, jump in bed, and hide under the warm covers until this whole nasty business was over.

As far as I was concerned, the hearing was unnecessary. In the months before the hearing, I prayed that the two sides would reach an agreement. I prayed that the Holy Spirit would intervene, softening hearts, restoring the love that had once been present, and causing the hearing to be canceled. I couldn't understand why this family member decided to inflict such heartache upon the rest of the family.

When it seemed that the hearing was indeed going to happen, my prayers changed. I began to ask God to allow confusion in the speech of those in the wrong and to give clarity of mind and strength to those in the right. But most of all, I asked for peace in my own heart. While I knew that God had everything under control, I did not feel the peace I so desperately wanted.

On the morning of the hearing, time ticked slowly by. The hands on the clock in the hall seemed to hardly budge. The case included so many witnesses that the judge asked us to wait patiently as she located a larger courtroom. Lawyers and witnesses for both sides stood in the hall together. No one spoke. We stared at the floor, the ceiling, the artwork on the walls—anything to avoid eye contact. My stomach felt as if I had eaten a bowl of rocks for breakfast, and I wanted to scream, "Can't we all just get along?"

These people had taken an oath to be truthful, and they were not. Was God listening to this at all?

The judge finally escorted us to a large room. After the first witness swore to tell the truth "so help me, God," the judge said he didn't need to add that last part.

My heart sank. I wondered where God was. It seemed that even the judge had thrown him out of the courtroom.

The lack of honesty I heard throughout the testimony saddened me.

These people had taken an oath to be truthful, and they were not. Was God listening to this at all?

After three hours we received a ten-minute recess. I reached for my purse and saw my Bible. Peeking out of a corner of my purse was the small New Testament with Psalms I always carry.

As I reached for it, I prayed, *Give me comfort, God. The world has forgotten you and the meaning of truth. I need you to speak to me right now.*

When I pulled my Bible from my purse in that courtroom it fell open to Psalm 26. My attitude began to change as I read the chapter:

"Vindicate me, O LORD, for I have led a blameless life; I have trusted in the LORD without wavering" (v. 1, NIV). Immediately I asked God to forgive my lack of trust. He was there with me all the time—I had no reason to fear or question his methods.

"Your love is ever before me, and I walk continually in your truth. I do not sit with deceitful men, nor do I consort with hypocrites" (vv. 3–4). My head snapped up, and I looked across the room. Was I really reading this? I had specifically asked God for comfort in this tension-packed room, and he gave me this psalm! I looked back down and continued to read.

"Do not take away my soul along with sinners, my life with bloodthirsty men, in whose hands are wicked schemes, whose right hands are full of bribes. But I lead a blameless life; redeem me and be merciful to me. My feet stand on level ground; in the great assembly I will praise the LORD" (vv. 9–12).

Gratitude swept over me like a cool breeze. The stifling stress began to melt away. I shared Psalm 26 with my husband and Deena. And I stopped shaking. God had given me the peace I so desperately needed.

When the recess ended, the attorneys for both sides approached the bench and spoke to the judge. Then they spoke to their clients. The two sides had reached an agreement, and the judge declared the hearing over. I didn't have to testify after all!

—*Carol Fielding*

WHEN GOD BREAKS THROUGH

God uses his Word to speak to us, very directly sometimes. He can make himself known to his children when we are hurting. To some people, the Bible is only an old, dusty book with no relevance. However, when we ask God to speak and give us comfort, he often does so through the Bible, just as Carol opened his Word, and God "spoke" the words she needed through the inspired psalm of an ancient king who had also faced lies and injustice. Carol may have read those words many times before, but at her moment of need God directed her to those words again, for he knew they would bring the comfort and peace she craved. The author of the book of Hebrews wrote, "The word of God is living and powerful" (Hebrews 4:12, NKJV). Far from being irrelevant, the Bible lives and speaks to God's people. When you open his Word, you place yourself at the feet of the Almighty God, ready to listen to his message to you.

MY CHALLENGE

Do you regularly open your Bible, or does it sit and collect dust? Challenge yourself to read your Bible on a regular basis. Look on the Internet for a reading plan to use, or begin with reading Proverbs, one chapter per day for a month. If you already read your Bible regularly, challenge yourself by reading God's Word in a different translation. When you open God's Word, he will speak to you through its pages— providing just what you need when you need it. Like Carol, you might even find what you need when you least expect it!

31 HUGE AND SCARY
Remembering How Big God Is

"*Wow!* How do you keep it all together? Your plate is so full!"

That's one of the highest compliments a person can give or receive in suburban Chicago, where busyness is celebrated. If you have free time, something is wrong with you. The most venerated people are those teetering on the edge of a breakdown.

I used to be a victim of that schedule-until-death-illness-or-major-catastrophe-strike, mentality, where the focus is on what you do, not on who you are. But no more.

We were studying the Book of Numbers at church, following the Israelites' journey after they were delivered from Egypt. God did amazing things that showed his ability to care for his people, but the Israelites always seemed to forget that as soon as the next problem came up. One week the message was about how some of them responded when they saw the promised land of Canaan, something akin to, "It's an amazing country, but the people are *huge.*"

How dumb could those Israelites be? God had just led them out of Egypt, drowned everyone who pursued them, miraculously fed them all the way across the desert, and brought them exactly where he'd promised. God was big enough to do all that. But the Israelites thought the Canaanites were too big and scary for them to conquer? *Silly Israelites.*

Church was over, and life went on. My life, as usual, was overly busy. I had a PDA task list two screens long and enough e-mail and phone calls to challenge the most competent time manager. One of my biggest worries that week was how I could accomplish all I needed to do. I found myself in the same conversation with almost anyone I talked to.

"How are you?" someone would ask.

"Busy," I'd say. "You?"

"Me too."

"Yeah. Tell me about it." Then I'd list some of the many items on my plate, watching to see how long it took for their eyes to fill with admiration or at least sympathy. Sometimes it took only a couple of

items, but with other people I needed to recite a litany of my day to get a response.

Some people tried to bring me back to reality, reminding me that God always provides or that I would accomplish what really mattered. I got annoyed with those people. Who were they to try to minimize my stress? I was the one who had so much to do that I could talk about it for hours!

Then I reread in my Bible about the silly Israelites. One sentence jumped out at me: "But the people living there are powerful, and their cities and towns are fortified and very large" (Numbers 13:28, NLT). The Israelites didn't think they'd be able to handle the Canaanites, which was smart, but they also didn't trust God, who could definitely handle the situation for them.

For some reason those three words—"but the people"—stayed with me. They sounded so whiny, so distrusting, so . . . familiar.

I realized that I sounded that way. My "but the people" was instead "but my schedule" or "but my commitments" or "but I'm *busy*." I had considered my overly booked schedule (which was, to a great degree, a problem of my own making) too much for God to handle.

My schedule didn't seem like such a big deal anymore. I resolved to never again torment anyone with a list of my activities, and I also determined to trust God to help me accomplish what I truly needed to do.

I got annoyed with those people. Who were they to try to minimize my stress?

My schedule is still full, but I've learned that the God who helped the Israelites overcome those big, scary Canaanites can also help me manage my big, scary tasks. With his help, I can do all he has for me to do. And that's a relief.

—*Heather Pleier*

WHEN GOD BREAKS THROUGH

We live in a busy, busy world. Too often our busyness is almost a competition: "Look how busy I am! I have a PDA, and my cell phone constantly rings. I'm busier than you are."

Do we think that the busiest person wins? Does that ringing cell phone make us feel important? Consider what Jesus would be like if he lived in our world. Would you see him constantly interrupting his conversations to answer his cell phone? Would he endlessly check his PDA and scamper around the Judean countryside trying to meet appointments? Hardly. Jesus had time to be with the people who came each day and needed him. He wasn't overscheduled; he was free to take the time to heal the leper or to have an impromptu dinner with Matthew or Zacchaeus. It's OK to be organized. And it's certainly OK to be busy. Just don't let your busyness become an idol in your life—like you have to show off how active you are. And don't let it hinder you from being there for the people who need you.

MY CHALLENGE

Look at all your activities. Are you proud of your busyness? Are you on overdrive to the point that you can't be there for the people closest to you? How can you begin to pare back to bring balance to your life? And for the activities that remain, ask the Lord to help you accomplish all you need to do. As God promised his servant Zerubbabel, "Not by might nor by power, but by my Spirit," (Zechariah 4:6, NIV). God is big enough to handle even *your* busy schedule!

32 UPROOTED
Finding God's Peace in Change

"There!" I exclaimed as I patted fresh dirt around the plants I'd just deposited into the soil on each side of the birdbath. I envisioned sitting in my breakfast nook, gazing at lush greenery, little birds hiding among the pink flowers and dashing out for a sip of water or a morning bath. I couldn't wait to enjoy such a wonderfully peaceful scene.

So different from the turmoil and stress in the rest of my life! I thought.

My husband and I were facing difficult decisions about moving our family for a new job opportunity. We had just come home to familiarity, comfort, and friends after two years overseas, and I wasn't ready to relocate again.

I hated thinking about all the changes another move would require: leaving friends behind, making new ones, changing schools, helping the children adjust, finding health care providers. I didn't want to leave my elderly parents behind either.

Our debates about moving continued for weeks. One morning as I gazed out the window in the breakfast nook, praying for comfort and direction concerning the ever pending decision, I realized my peaceful backyard scene was also not progressing as planned. I could barely see the birdbath.

That's odd, I thought. I'd already planted spirea in the front yard. It had been so beautiful that I'd decided to repeat the performance in the backyard. But this plant looked stalkier and taller than what was in my front yard. *Oh, no! I must have planted the wrong thing,* I realized.

I went outside and double-checked the tags: spiraea—that can grow to be eight feet tall! Same name, different variety. Not only were my plants hardy, but they were also aggressive, conquering my entire flower bed. "Well, you're beautiful and you'll definitely have a place in my yard, but you can't stay where you are," I muttered to the stalks as I started digging. The spiraea had certainly thrived; the roots were deep and interwoven. I tried to reach every wandering root and preserve as much of the root balls as possible.

This is harder than I expected! I thought as I wiped the sweat off my face. *I'm probably stressing out the plants too.*

"You'll be fine," I told the plants. "You'll like your new home, and I promise to take good care of you."

I kept prodding. The roots seemed obstinate and uncooperative. "Come on out of there now, please. You're just hurting yourself."

> *My own roots were too deeply planted in my little world. I was so comfortable that* any *change would be painful.*

The relocation took hours of difficult labor. As I burrowed in the soil, I contemplated our family's situation.

Why can't we just stay here? Why does my life need to be upset?

Suddenly I stood and laughed out loud. Of course! Moving my plants was an effective and loving way for God to show me that my own roots were too deeply planted in my little world. I was so comfortable that *any* change would be painful.

I am sure that God met me in my garden. No beams of light, no rushing wind, no blazing fire—only sweat and worry and frustration. And then clarity. Home had become my security, and my focus was more on that than on God and his guidance.

What an uprooting would look like, I didn't know, but I understood that some sort of change was on its way, and that the change was coming from God.

A move from our present home might still be in our future, but I am certain that God is with me regardless of my circumstances. So I want to be hardy—able to thrive even during difficult times.

—Gloria Spielman

WHEN GOD BREAKS THROUGH

We find security in our relationship with God by listening to his guidance and finding contentment with where he takes us. No matter what directives he gives us, his consistent message is that he is with us. Through all changes and every adjustment, he is with us. Our job is to hold this life loosely and to cling to him. In writing to his protégé, Paul encouraged Timothy to persevere in his faith like a soldier who often must experience sacrifice and endure hardships to achieve goals. Paul wrote, "As Christ's soldier, do not let yourself become tied up in the affairs of this life, for then you cannot satisfy the one who has enlisted you in his army" (2 Timothy 2:4, NLT).

MY CHALLENGE

Think about a change you are facing or have recently faced. What circumstances were involved? How do you feel about and respond to changes? Ask God to show you what lessons you can learn from your experiences.

33 UNDERWATER RESCUE

Giving Credit to the Real Superhero

Our son Tommy was four years old, and every ounce of his being was buzzing with excitement over the prospect of joining his mom and me on a church canoe trip. You would have thought he was going on a space shuttle launch. Little did he realize that getting into a wobbly canoe with his uncoordinated dad presented only slightly less of a risk.

After two hours of paddling, forging a half-dozen rapids, and capsizing an equal number of times (we called it "spontaneous swimming"), Tommy and my wife and I were soaked, laughing, and hungry. We steered over to join the group taking a snack break on the sandy riverbank. I got out, pulled the boat up near the bank, and began to help Tommy. As he climbed out of the canoe, his right foot brushed against the edge of the boat. One of his new "big-boy water shoes," purchased that morning especially for this trip (and which he had proudly modeled for everyone, including a tollbooth attendant), fell off and sank quickly in the dark water.

The three of us stared in disbelief as the shoe disappeared.

Who makes these lousy things? They're water shoes. Shouldn't they float?

Tears filled Tommy's blue eyes as he mourned the loss of his prized possession. When I explained that we probably would not be able to find his shoe, he openly cried. The swift current, murky water, and steep drop-off just beyond the shore would make finding the shoe nearly impossible.

Saddened to see my boy so upset, I promised to try to defy the odds and the power of the river to get it back. I was fully committed to this underwater recovery expedition. I didn't want to shatter Tommy's belief that I possessed superhuman powers.

My wife and friends tried to convince me that the situation was hopeless because of the water conditions, the odds against finding a small shoe in a big river, and the fact that I can barely find my car keys in my own pocket. But I immediately saw the irresistible opportunity to be a superhero, and against their advice I dived in.

As I went under, I realized that the water was deeper than any pool I had ever been in and that salt and mud stung like hot sauce eyedrops. Finding the shoe by sight was out of the question. Maybe my wife and friends were right. But they had underestimated both my stubbornness and my desire for hero status.

The water was deeper than any pool I had ever been in and that salt and mud stung like hot sauce eyedrops.

Coming up for air I told the crowd that had gathered that the situation looked bleak. Then with a bit of fanfare, I went down a second time. As I reached bottom my hand brushed against something that felt strangely familiar, like a small water shoe—I knew the feeling well, as I had held the shoe in my hands just hours earlier at the sporting goods store wondering if I should pay way too much for it. Yes, it was Tommy's shoe! I jetted victoriously toward the sunlit surface.

This is pretty incredible! If I milk it, this could be really impressive.

I decided to do just that. Instead of coming up with the good news, I hid the shoe under the water. Again my wife and friends pleaded with me to give up, but I would hear none of it and told them I was going down for one more try. With a dramatic flair usually reserved for Olympic swimmers, I dived to the bottom a third time (no easy task, since my midsection is naturally buoyant). All I had to do was wait underwater, resurface, and make a grand presentation of the shoe.

I reached bottom and stayed there until I thought my lungs would burst. Then I blasted to the surface. The shoe in my raised fist broke the water first. If this were a movie, the soundtrack would be swelling to an emotional crescendo here. As the water drained from my ears, I heard the gasps of disbelief and roar of applause from my wife and friends. Tommy was beaming. He was never so proud of his dad who had just accomplished the impossible. I ate it up. It was perfect—almost.

It was at that moment that Tommy said something that pierced my heart. "I was praying for you, Dad, and I knew that God would help you find it."

My boy was faithful. I was not. I wandered off and sat alone on the shore, pondering why I had handled the situation the way I did. God had allowed me to restore a little boy's happiness, and I had stolen the glory. How many other times had I gritted my teeth, worked with all my might, and basked in my own glory? Too many.

When we got home, I told Tommy the truth about my prideful performance. It didn't faze him. He had his shoe back, he still loved me, he still believed I was the strongest man in the world, and he still had his childishly unshakable faith in God. And I realized how much sweeter it is to celebrate the wonderful power of God than the self-imagined superpowers of a middle-aged dad.

—Tom Burggraf

WHEN GOD BREAKS THROUGH

As the Scriptures say, "If anyone is going to boast, let him boast about what the Lord has done and not about himself" (2 Corinthians 10:17, TLB).

Whether we face challenges at home, work, school, or on the playing field, the question is the same: Will we show the world that *we* can do the impossible, or that our God can? The choice is ours with everything we attempt, every day. We must beware while paddling the river of life that when we take the glory for ourselves, the world and sometimes even the church will applaud. And in the end we will have lost much more than a little boy's overpriced water shoe. We will have lost part of our witness, part of our faith, and part of the delight of faithfulness. However, when we give God all the glory, Jesus smiles, applauds, and brings us out of the water with deep and lasting joy. Which will you choose?

MY CHALLENGE

Jesus told his followers that those who did good deeds in secret would be rewarded (Matthew 6:3–4). What good deed can you do today that no one but you and God will know about?

34 THE LEAST, THE LOST, AND THE LONELY

Discovering Jesus in a Garbage Dump

Rhada lives in Mokattam, a garbage dump populated by 10,000 people outside Cairo, Egypt. Its people are hungry, isolated, and poor beyond imagination. Slow-moving donkeys, disease-infested rats, and mangy dogs fill the streets and share the homes of this seemingly godforsaken village. The pervasive smell is putrid, rising up from this city stained by feces, litter, and sadness. Rhada's family, along with the other inhabitants, earn their livelihoods collecting rubbish from the city streets. They eat the scraps of food they find; they save the dirty, used plastics for their own use.

I met 10-year-old Rhada, her dirty, brown hair matted against her worn-out face, when I served on a short-term Youth for Christ mission trip to build a church in Mokattam.

Every day our team walked through Rhada's neighborhood and past her home on the way to our worksite. We gagged at the intolerable odor, so we covered our faces with small pieces of cloth. Temperatures rose above 110 degrees making us tired and cranky. We hoped to demonstrate the love of Christ to people who were scarcely making life work, but we were failing miserably.

The cloths over our faces were rude and inconsiderate, insulating us from

Rhada and her family and all her friends who lived in the heat and stench day in and day out. Good intentions aside, I had missed the point of our trip completely until I met Rhada and noticed her bare feet.

The day I quit holding a cloth over my mouth, I also began to stop and say hello to her, wishing we spoke a common language. I sat on her porch while a translator helped us communicate small phrases accompanied by awkward facial expressions.

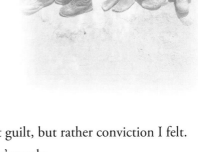

Rhada was shy. I was too. But humility, melancholy, and joy flooded my heart the moment Rhada smiled at me. Conviction followed quickly. Rhada had no shoes. Her feet were caked with dirt from the littered ground. My closet at home contained at least a dozen pairs of shoes. It wasn't guilt, but rather conviction I felt. God used Rhada to remind me of Jesus' words:

> "For I was hungry and you gave me food, I was thirsty and you gave me drink, I was a stranger and you welcomed me, I was naked and you clothed me, I was sick and you visited me, I was in prison and you came to me." Then the righteous will answer him, saying, "Lord, when did we see you hungry and feed you, or thirsty and give you drink? And when did we see you a stranger and welcome you, or naked and clothe you? And when did we see you sick or in prison and visit you?" And the King will answer them, "Truly, I say to you, as you did it to one of the least of these my brothers, you did it to me." (Matthew 25:35–40, ESV).

Giving Rhada a pair of my shoes was the easy part. The difficulty was realizing that Jesus was actually receiving the gift in a deeply spiritual way. Jesus was going to wear my old tennis shoes. Weird, huh? But it changed me.

Now needy strangers on street corners receive less judgment and more tangible help from me. Family members who are hurting receive more of my time and less of my anger and impatience. Struggling friends gain my listening ear more quickly.

Every time I offer something of myself, Jesus is the recipient of that love, money, time, or concern. It's true. Gifts offered in Jesus' name are like gifts given twice.

Rhada had no shoes. Her feet were caked with dirt from the littered ground.

God broke through to me that summer day in the garbage dump outside Cairo. I wish I had given more. I want Jesus to have my best shoes. I know he is able to receive whatever I give, and since that day the desire to give generously, lavishly, even indiscriminately is growing in my soul.

And Rhada's picture is on the wall of my office to remind me.

—*Jennifer Morgan*

WHEN GOD BREAKS THROUGH

Jesus told his disciples that the poor would always be around (Matthew 26:11). Sadly we see evidence of that with every homeless person we pass on the street. But *poor* does not always mean someone destitute. Poor can mean someone discouraged or isolated. Many times, we fear reaching out, thinking our efforts too little or too late. But like Jennifer, we need not fear reaching out. In a parable Jesus said, "I tell you the truth, whatever you did for one of the least of these brothers of mine, you did for me" (Matthew 25:40, NIV). *Whatever you did.* This could mean offering a prayer for someone or giving the shoes off your feet as Jennifer did. It could also mean spending time with a lonely or special needs child. Whatever is done in Jesus' name is done for him as well.

MY CHALLENGE

Who are "the least of these" in your community? School? Workplace? You don't have to wait until the holidays to give to the ones who can give nothing in return. With your family, brainstorm ways to be creative in your giving. Giving doesn't always have to mean money. Perhaps you can give time to help in a homeless shelter or an orphanage.

35 THE POWER OF LOVE
Dismantling the Walls Around People's Hearts

When I first met 17-year-old Stephen, he looked ready for a photo shoot for an upscale clothes catalogue. He had that dour, bored look of the models displayed in the mall's store. And he was angry—his mom had forced him to come to church to talk with me.

My staff and I were preparing to take hundreds of teenagers from Portland, Oregon, on a ministry trip to Southern California. We hoped they would encounter Jesus in some new way. In the midst of our harried preparations, Stephen's mom begged us to convince her son to go on this trip. I walked outside to talk with Stephen.

I stuck out my hand in greeting. Stephen looked at me—wearing board shorts and sandals—with surprise. Still he kept his distance. His walls were definitely up, and they seemed made of bricks.

I laid out the plan, simple and straightforward—this was what we were embarking on, and he was welcome to join us. He snorted a dismissing comment back at me before I finished my short infomercial.

"Up to you," I said. "No pressure. I promise we won't put you in a closet until you repent. Not until the last night anyway."

His eyes searched mine to see if I was serious or just brazen enough to tease him. I gave him a slight smile, waved to his mom, and returned to my preparations.

Two days later Stephen showed up for the trip. I gave him the standard guy greeting—a slight up nod of the chin—and went on about my work. I didn't want him to think he was my "project," even though he was— especially because I loved the ones with attitude! I noticed that he had broken his arm since I met him and was wearing a cast. *He must want to be here,* I thought, *not to let that easy excuse keep him away.*

I worked to make small talk over the next few days. He rebuffed me often, but weakened as he watched me with others and learned I wasn't that scary. I also showed interest in his world: surfing. I don't surf. I'd look like a polar bear on a sheet of plywood! But I faked it enough to get him talking—it was his turf and he felt safe.

My friend Darren was one of our speakers. Stephen connected with Darren's punk style and straight-up engagement of life and faith questions. But Stephen wanted us to know he wasn't buying it.

"Don't think just because we can talk, I am becoming one of those Christians," Stephen stated flatly. The brick walls were still strong, but we did keep talking. Each night he moved from the group of hundreds of teenagers in worship to sit at the back with some of his new friends.

During our trip we planned a day at the beach as a reward for busy days of ministry. I found Stephen walking down the beach alone. We walked and talked. He stuck his toe in the "water" of friendship with me and felt he could surf it. I sensed a bit more openness and decided to go for it: I asked what he thought about God.

"I'm really the only person I can trust, man," he said.

The wall went back up. "I'm really the only person I can trust, man," he said. He told me how God had "dissed" so many people he knew. I reflected that it's funny how self-absorbed teenagers suddenly develop deep concern for others in far-fetched places when the subject of God comes up!

I said the short prayer so often demonstrated in the Bible, "Lord, help me," as I tried to read Stephen and form my next words. I used my favorite tool—silence. I leaned on the pier railing and stared at the surfers. Stephen also remained silent.

"Stephen, I am so sorry," I finally said. "Someone has really hurt you in the past."

His eyes instantly softened and then broke contact. He looked to his left, away from me, and stared at the open sea. I can still hear the sea and the birds, see the glaring sunlight, smell the air of that moment. Several seconds seemed an eternity, and then knowing I was watching, he nodded his head.

God himself broke into Stephen's heart. The love of God is so strong that it can withstand rage, indictment, doubts, questions, and renunciations—and still be there. People are saved when they encounter the love of Christ who doesn't wait to love them until they recant their arguments against God.

Stephen and I talked for a long time that afternoon. God moved kingdoms that week: Stephen's angry eyes softened and his physical countenance even changed.

Over the weeks, months, and years since, Stephen has become a man who still rejects religious veneer (and I applaud that), but who passionately loves God and sacrificially loves others. As a Marine helicopter mechanic on deployments around the world, including Afghanistan, he continues to care for others in a strong but steady reflection of Jesus.

He's proof that God's love dismantles brick walls.

—Mike Brantley

WHEN GOD BREAKS THROUGH

We won't break through people's hard hearts by knowing the ins and outs of every world religion or the zingers that can end each argument against Christianity. God alone can break down those walls. No number of our convincing words can make the difference. Mike discovered that getting through to Stephen meant listening, caring, and waiting for God's timing. The people around us ache for a better reality (hope), long for something to live for (faith), and crave unconditional acceptance (love). We can show them what Jesus is like when we act as his hands and feet on earth. We befriend, we listen, we care, we're there. We love, and we let God break through even the thickest brick walls. God promises, "I will give you a new heart and put a new spirit in you; I will remove from you your heart of stone and give you a heart of flesh" (Ezekiel 36:26, NIV). And when those walls come down, we'll be ready to walk with that person into the kingdom.

MY CHALLENGE

Look around you. Is someone right under your nose searching for God? Pray for that person regularly. Look for ways you can be Jesus' representative to that person. Remember, you don't have to be the one to convince someone of the truth of your faith. You only need to reach out in love. God will do the rest.

36 My Father's Taillights
Following as God Leads

I was tense for sure. Alone in my car, it didn't seem like enough that Dad was in front of me guiding me home from my freshman year at college. This was my first long trip behind the wheel and I was filled with irrational fears: What if I got lost? What if the car broke down and I couldn't get Dad's attention? What if I couldn't keep up with him?

The weather didn't help. Between the misting rain, fog, and condensation on my windshield I couldn't see clearly. The wind picked up. I clutched the steering wheel a little tighter. I was already miserable and we still had three hours to go.

At least Dad's willing to help me, I thought, trying to encourage myself. My little Volkswagen couldn't hold all my belongings, and I had always hated to travel alone. So when my exams were over, Dad came with his truck. He loaded my belongings in the back, and we started home with him leading the way. I had felt better as we started out because I wouldn't be alone on the roads that night, but Dad liked to drive the back roads so I followed him through territory I didn't know. I turned on the radio and tried to distract myself from my worries, but to no avail. Why was I so worked up over this trip home?

I desperately wanted to tell him I was scared to death.

We finally stopped for dinner and I was glad to be out of the car.

"How are you doing so far?" Dad asked. "How's the car running?"

"Everything's fine," I lied. "I'm OK."

I desperately wanted to tell him I was scared to death. I wished I could beg him to drive my car for me and let me sit in the passenger seat watching the trees go by. I didn't want to deal with the rain or the wind or the foggy window or the traffic or the curvy roads.

Take over for me, Dad, would you please? This is too much for me and I can't handle it, I said in my mind.

But I kept the actual words to myself. I realized how silly that would sound, and I felt childish for being scared. I didn't want Dad to be disappointed in me. Besides, both of us had to drive so we could get both vehicles home.

Back in my car, once again braving the weather, the traffic, the roads, and the irrational fears, I wished there was an easier way. But that's when I saw them, gleaming back at me—my father's taillights. Though they'd been there all day, I suddenly noticed them. Bright red and glowing like two friendly beacons. I felt like a sailor at sea, dripping wet and fighting the waves, who suddenly spots the lighthouse! I couldn't see street signs and sometimes not even the line in the middle of the road, but I could see my father's taillights. So I followed them all the way home—along those dark, unfamiliar roads, around the curves, through the rain.

Lying in bed that night, I thought about those taillights. What would I have done without them? What would I have done without my dad leading the way safely home? That night as I thought about my fears of the day, I realized that God had been reaching down to me with those lights. I knew I had to grow up, but I had never taken challenges head-on—I was more likely to hide my head in a pillow! So God had stepped up the challenge. No one else could take the wheel for me. The roads could not be straightened; the darkness wouldn't become daytime. I had to drive, but God gave me lights to follow.

This seemed to be a fitting lesson that has stayed with me. The roads may be curvy, the weather inclement, the way dark and dreary. But I can rest in the fact that I can follow my heavenly Father. Life will be an exciting adventure, no matter where he leads me.

—*Alison Simpson*

WHEN GOD BREAKS THROUGH

What a comfort to know that we can follow Jesus. Not only does he know the end from the beginning, he also wants to guide us through the pathways of our lives. Like a shepherd, Jesus leads us, his sheep, watching over us, making sure we're cared for, giving protection and help. He said, "My sheep hear My voice, and I know them, and they follow Me" (John 10:27, NKJV). Alison experienced this as she followed the taillights on her father's truck. She knew her father wouldn't lead her astray; he wouldn't try to lose her or cause her harm. He loved her and wanted to bring her safely home. He couldn't drive the car for her, but he could be the guide. As God's child, you are promised guidance from the Good Shepherd. He will guide you; you just need to watch for the taillights and stay close.

MY CHALLENGE

What unfamiliar roads are you traveling on? Where do you need God's guidance most? Write down exactly what you need from God, and then offer it to him in prayer. Remember James' words while you pray:

> If any of you lacks wisdom, he should ask God, who gives generously to all without finding fault, and it will be given to him. But when he asks, he must believe and not doubt, because he who doubts is like a wave of the sea, blown and tossed by the wind. That man should not think he will receive anything from the Lord (James 1:5–7, NIV).

Ask with confidence for God's guidance—and he will generously give you what you need.

37 A SONG IN THE DARK

Finding Courage to Face Our Fears

"No, Mommy, no!" my son shrieked as I tried to coax him down the long, dark corridor to get to the bathroom and to bed by himself.

Kids sure can be irrational, I grumbled inside. My baby daughter was nursing and had just fallen asleep. I pleaded with my son, encouraged him, and even mildly threatened, but he just clung to my leg, paralyzed with fear. Isaac is autistic and it's difficult to reason with him.

I remembered a song we sang the day before in Sunday school. "Come on, Isaac, sing with me and march!" Surprised, Isaac let go of my leg. I sang in the quietest voice I could muster, so I wouldn't wake my daughter, "I am not afraid. I am not afraid. For I know God's on my side."

"I remember that song, Mommy!" Isaac exclaimed, and began to sing with me. By the second verse his tears were gone, and he was marching around the room. Still singing, he marched into the dark and turned on the light in his room while I laid my sleeping daughter in bed. Relieved at finding a way to calm his fears, I smiled as I helped Isaac get ready for bed.

Months later my husband left me, and I reacted very much like my son. "No, God, no!" I cried, clinging to the familiar, paralyzed with fear.

I knew I had few options. I was alone with two small children and could not continue living at my sister's house in Seattle. But the thought of moving away from my family and living on my own terrified me.

My friend in Illinois encouraged me to move to Chicago. "So many people here want to help you," she said. She and her friends were even collecting furniture for me. But I would never make it through the winters there, and the only person I knew in Chicago was my best friend from college days. What if she moved? How could I survive with a toddler and an autistic child? Leaving my family just didn't make sense, but God seemed to clearly nudge me to go.

"God, you seem to be leading me, but I don't know!" I cried aloud. "I can't make these decisions alone. Help me!" I laid my head in my arms, totally overwhelmed.

I don't know how long I sat there before I heard my son shouting, "Mommy, Mommy! Where are you?"

I entered the dark bedroom where he had been sleeping and tried to calm him, but he had awakened from a nightmare and was terrified. He stuck his fingers in his ears, a habit he often resorted to when he was afraid, and shrieked again, "Mommy, Mommy! Where are you?"

Months later, my husband left me, and I reacted very much like my son. "No, God, no!"

"Isaac, I am right here," I said. I picked him up and began to sing, "I am not afraid. I am not afraid. For I know God's on my side."

I sat for a while at Isaac's side in the dark after he fell asleep again. I felt a familiar nudge in my heart. Now that I was calm I sensed that God was using this experience to speak to me.

I've been acting like Isaac, haven't I, Lord? Shouting in the dark with my fingers in my ears.

"I am not afraid. I am not afraid. For I know God's on my side." The words washed over me as I knelt by my son and prayed.

Then I called my friend in Chicago. "We're coming!"

God was preparing a whole new life for us there. When I was afraid,

I only had to find a song in the dark, and my heavenly Father would be there to hold my hand.

—*Colleen Yang*

WHEN GOD BREAKS THROUGH

Being brave is not about getting rid of fear but about focusing the fear to become the adrenaline we need to face obstacles. Sometimes we are weak and cannot even get past the overwhelming fear. At this point we need to focus and release the fear to God.

This verse expresses part of the process of overcoming whatever blocks us: "So you should not be cowering like fearful slaves. You should behave instead like God's very own children, adopted into his family—calling him 'Father, dear Father'" (Romans 8:15, NLT).

First we need to be honest about our need and cry out to the Father. He then gives us the strength to hear him and focus on him. Though the feeling of fear may not leave, we find God's peace. Through this peace we may face the daunting situation ahead of us with confidence that God is with us and that with him we can overcome any circumstances.

MY CHALLENGE

Think of a song or hymn you can sing to redirect your mind on the Lord. The Bible offers so many verses about peace and resting in God. Look in a concordance or run a search on an online Bible. Ask the Lord to direct you to the verses you need and ask him what action you can take to face your fears.

38 CHANCE MEETING
Receiving God's Unexpected Provision

"I can't believe that guy has nothing better to do than read comic books," Dad mumbled under his breath as we left a darkened apartment. "He looks like he's 26 years old!"

My father had invested several hundred dollars in airfare and several days of his life to assure himself that I hadn't gone off the deep end. Right now in his eyes, the prognosis didn't look healthy!

Dad hadn't worried like this when I'd spent a year in Colombia, South America, on a short-term mission. He understood missions to other nations. However reaching out to the counterculture in America was something else. I'd been working in Chicago, doing coffeehouse evangelism for several years now, and that was unfamiliar territory to my dad. I'd let my appearance match that of those I ministered to, and my letters rarely mentioned Sunday school or youth group meetings. Dad wanted to see just what I was involved in, so he flew to Chicago to visit me.

His first two days of hanging out with me did little to bolster his confidence. When he got right up close to my world—so close he could smell it—it wasn't an inviting atmosphere for a strict pastor raised during the Depression and World War II.

Visiting my hirsute friends in their dirty but brightly painted apartments,

Dad sat on dingy couches next to stringy-haired adolescents who had handrolled cigarettes dangling from their lips. His attempts to exercise the social skills honed over decades failed miserably. Usually my friends greeted him superficially and then ignored him for the rest of our visit. In the hovels of my Chicago matrix of relationships, conversations were anything but sparkling on a hot summer afternoon, especially after a long hard night of partying.

"I wonder if anyone in that place *ever* empties that cat's litter box?" Dad muttered about our last visit.

Then a miracle happened. As we walked down the sidewalk, we passed a couple going the opposite direction.

"Oswaldo?" I yelled, astonished.

"Gino!" he called out at the same moment. We both spun around, incredulous.

Oswaldo was an elder in the church in Medellin, Colombia, where I had worked on my short-term mission. Now he was standing with his bride in front of me. How amazing that on a street in a city with three million people we saw each other.

"I didn't even know you were here!" I shouted in Spanish. Simultaneously he shouted that he and Maria had married and moved to the United States six months earlier. "Our apartment is only a block away. Please, please, come home with us now so we can visit!" they begged.

I translated all this for my dad, who already sensed that this experience would be different from those he'd been subject to for two days.

"Sure," he said. "If you want to go over to their place, let's go!"

My dad finally felt on familiar turf. Oswaldo told me about several young men I'd taken to church with me in Colombia who had become Christians after I left. I whooped at the news and translated it for Dad. Maria pulled out her wedding album to show him their pictures. Clearly she and Oswaldo were in love, but they were lonely, and my dad was just the kind of person they both needed to relate to at that moment. Nurturing a younger brother and sister in Christ—that was what Dad lived for, and he had finally found a way to do what he was good at on my territory.

His attempts to exercise the social skills honed over decades failed miserably.

The two hours we spent at Oswaldo and Maria's little love nest changed the atmosphere for the rest of my dad's visit. He walked out of there beaming, and I was thrilled by the coincidence, until I realized it wasn't a coincidence.

Oswaldo and I met each other on the street that day, two people out of three million, because the Holy Spirit guided our paths together. Through that encounter my dad saw a completely different picture of me that day—different even from the formal "mission reports" that I would give in church. From then on we were not only father and son, but also "brothers" in ministry.

—*Gene Smillie*

WHEN GOD BREAKS THROUGH

The apostle Paul had learned through his experiences—including imprisonments, beatings, false accusations, hunger, shipwrecks, and other hardships—that God always provided whatever he needed. Based on that, Paul was equally confident that God would provide for us. "And this same God who takes care of me will supply all your needs from his glorious riches, which have been given to us in Christ Jesus" (Philippians 4:19, NLT).

God knew that Oswaldo and Maria needed companionship that day. He also knew that Gene and his father needed to understand each other in the light of ministry. God helps out where and when we least expect it. And he will provide for us in ways that exceed our greatest imaginings.

MY CHALLENGE

What do you need from God today? Read Paul's stirring closing prayer of praise to God in Ephesians 3:20: "Now glory be to God! By his mighty power at work within us, he is able to accomplish infinitely more than we would ever dare to ask or hope" (NLT). Based on these powerful words, tell God what you need and wait for his provision.

39 IT'S NOT FAIR
Accepting Life's Disappointments

"Mr. Ezell, you satisfactorily defended your thesis. Congratulations. Good job," said the supervisory professor.

My heart leaped with joy at reaching this milestone. The past nine months had all led to this day. If I passed the oral defense, I would be allowed to enter the PhD program, which was my ultimate objective. The school administration had assured me that I would certainly be admitted into the doctoral program if I completed the master's work.

To the best of my ability, I had answered questions and defended the conclusions of my thesis for two hours. And now the taste of victory was sweet.

"However," the supervisory professor continued, "the graduate committee has rejected your application into the doctoral program. We wanted to tell you personally before the rejection letter arrived in the mail. The doctoral program requires that you earn all As in the master of theology classes. You unfortunately earned two Bs."

Like a guillotine on a helpless victim, those words sliced into my heart, cutting off my future in one fell swoop.

With my eye on the doctoral program, I had completed the master of theology course work in nine months. Most students take 12 to 18 months. No school administrator ever told me that I had to receive all As in the master's program to be admitted to doctoral study.

How can they do this? Dizzy and sick, I fought to keep tears away.

After leaving the building, I raced into our townhouse and slammed the door. "It's not fair! It's just not fair!"

Many times I had counseled people, "Life isn't fair." Now as I tried to swallow those three words myself, they went down hard and bitter. Saint Augustine was right, "God had one son on earth without sin, but never one without suffering."

For three years my wife and I had planned and saved and given up so much for this lifelong dream of mine. Now what would we do? *How could God let this happen?* I questioned.

The next day I went to the hospital to visit my friend's mother. She was dying. The doctors knew it; the family knew it. She was a relatively young woman; her long illness and impending death were not fair. But there in that hospital room, as the family reflected on her life, they thanked God for his graciousness. "God has been good. He gave us nine unexpected years with her," they recounted.

Like a guillotine on a helpless victim, those words sliced into my heart, cutting off my future.

God, are you speaking to me? I wondered.

I left the hospital with my shoulders a little straighter, aware that the nightmare of my rejection had begun a slow turn toward dawn.

I guess difficulty and discouragement can either destroy me or define me, Lord, I realized.

This experience, as painful as it was, would not sever my relationship with God. Instead it would be a magnet drawing me to him and his plans for me. Life isn't fair, but God is.

—*Rick Ezell*

ALONG THE WAY

WHEN GOD BREAKS THROUGH

Through our disappointments we can realize that even when life is unfair, God is good. As we take our eyes off the circumstances and focus on God, we realize afresh that God knows what's best for us. That doesn't mean we won't experience pain. But in the midst of distress, we can have faith that God is at work for our ultimate good. God's primary goal for our lives is that we become conformed to his Son, not that we find comfort in our situations. The problem for us is that we only see in the dimension of time, while God is weaving a tapestry out of our lives with eternal purposes.

MY CHALLENGE

If you are experiencing rejection and disappointment, consider what God might be teaching you or what message he may be trying to tell you. Through your painful rejection—a divorce, a job loss, or losing a friendship you'd counted on—God may be preparing you for something significant. Reflect on the promise God gave to the Israelites—a promise he said would be fulfilled after they passed through years of struggles: "'For I know the plans I have for you,' declares the LORD, 'plans to prosper you and not to harm you, plans to give you hope and a future'" (Jeremiah 29:11, NIV). How can this promise change your view of your current situation?

40 THE ART OF TOILET SCRUBBING

Learning Humility in Menial Tasks

I can make a mean cappuccino. I discovered this talent when I took on a second job as a barista at Starbucks. I quickly learned I could also pump out lattes, mochas, and Americanos like nobody's business. But fulfilling people's caffeine—and decaf—needs just wasn't enough. I wondered what I was really doing with my life.

My other job—assistant sales coordinator at a publishing house—sounded impressive but was in reality just an entry-level position. Great people, great environment, great hours, and menial tasks—mostly fill-in-the-gaps work for the higher-ups in my department. I made thousands of mailing labels, entered pages upon pages of data, and printed off a truckload of form letters.

I was thankful for both jobs—they paid the rent and helped put food on the table, but they were nothing spectacular.

"All work is honorable work if it's moral and helps your family," my mom had always told me. But I was part of the "you can do anything" generation, and we grew to believe, starting in kindergarten, that we should only do work that we love. Unfortunately reality was much harsher than kindergarten dreams for me and for most of my highly educated, college graduate friends.

Among my four college roommates, only Jess had a real—but

ALONG THE WAY

low-paying—job as a teacher. Emily had worked as a camp counselor and was trying to save enough money to move to Los Angeles and break into the film business. Jen was coaching soccer and working construction, and Kayla had started four years of dental school. Combined we had college degrees that cost more than $400,000. During our first year out of college, after Kayla's tuition bills were subtracted, it looked like we would net a combined total of $3,000!

Sometimes dreams are just that—dreams.

Baristas have many tasks, including cleaning the bathroom. The glamorous barista also scrubs toilets. One day I came home feeling worthless and sat on the couch. I felt absolutely pitiful as a Christian and as a human being. I spent my days doing nothing particularly important. I was not ushering in the kingdom with trumpet blasts. I was not even talking with my coworkers about Christ because most were already believers. I was producing nothing of worth or value. I cried a little bit and waited for my husband, Michael, to come home so I could cry to him too.

The glamorous barista also scrubs toilets. . . . I came home feeling worthless . . .

Michael listened, hugged me, and told me what I did not want to hear—that he appreciated how hard I worked to help us stay afloat financially. I wanted him to tell me to quit, to throw down my apron and my envelopes and do whatever I wanted to do. But Michael hadn't gone to my kindergarten. He came from a real world. We both needed to work and I knew it.

I moped around for the next week, convinced I was missing out on my life's calling or—worse yet—my true purpose in life. I wasn't happy, so I concluded something must be wrong.

Then one gray Saturday afternoon, I read Romans 12:16, "Do not be haughty, but associate with the lowly" (ESV). The footnote pointed out that the verse could also be translated, "Give yourself over to humble tasks."

I grabbed a different translation of the Bible. The footnote there interpreted the verse to also mean, "Give yourself over to menial tasks" (NIV).

Sigh.

God had my attention. All the work I did was menial. I had been giving myself over to menial tasks for a month now. What was next?

Keep doing them, God said.

Great, I thought. *Just wonderful.*

Keep doing them, he said again. *But do them for me, not for you.*

Another sigh, and then the tears came, along with the realization of my selfish mindset. I was discontent not because my work was horrible but because I was focused on one thing—me. Why did I think I was above what I found myself doing?

So now I scrub toilets for Jesus. I told my husband once, deadly serious, that I pray hardest when I'm scrubbing the toilet bowls at work, saying over and over, "I do this for you, Jesus, I do this for you." Jesus is the only one I do that work for, the only one completely worthy of *all* of the work I do, no matter what it might be.

Jesus said he'd reward us anytime we give a cup of water in his name (Matthew 10:42). I'm learning the same holds true with a mean cappuccino.

—*Ann Swindell*

WHEN GOD BREAKS THROUGH

Whether your work feels high powered or lowly whether you're the president or the janitor whether you feel fulfilled or are just marking time, remember that God provides your work so you can serve others and honor him—and pay your bills! God reminds his children that ultimately we are to do all work for him and his glory. The apostle Paul wrote: "Work willingly at whatever you do, as though you were working for the Lord rather than for people" (Colossians 3:23, NLT). It can be difficult to feel valuable and to feel that you're honoring the Lord when you're not moving in the direction you dreamed of, when you're not using the gifts God has given you, or when you're not in the career you've prepared for. It's difficult to go to a job that you feel doesn't provide anything valuable to anyone. Regardless, God calls upon you to do your job well—with a smile on your face, to the best of your ability, and with integrity. When you approach your job with the attitude that God is your boss as well as your customer, you will find the motivation you need! And you might just learn to like what you're doing. You might even find hidden blessings as well.

MY CHALLENGE

Try doing every part of your job today as though God is right there with you. When your day ends, consider how that change in perspective affected your attitude toward your job. How will it make a difference when the alarm goes off tomorrow?

41 CROWDS, FISH OIL, AND EGO

Letting God Take Us Where He Wants Us

Destination: Bolivia.

That was where I planned to be when I graduated from college. It made sense. When I was in high school, I traveled on several mission trips—performing music in Italy, building houses in Mexico, and serving with a medical mission team in Bolivia. Each trip was focused on sharing God's love and serving others' physical needs. They were amazing trips, and I thought the lifestyle of missions fit me perfectly.

I especially felt at home in Bolivia. I was studying the language at college, I liked the food, the landscape was gorgeous, and I could relate to the people. It made sense that if God wanted me to serve him overseas, Bolivia should be my destination, and with my college courses, I was on track for that goal.

Then my university had a week with a world outreach focus. I decided to help organize and run the event.

One day when I was walking through the booths that lined the display area, I noticed that no one was talking with the representative for an organization that worked in China. I felt this might be awkward for the rep, so as one of the leaders, I felt it was my responsibility to go to his booth and talk with him.

"Are you interested in going to China?" Scott asked as I greeted him.

"You know, I don't think I'll end up there," I said diplomatically, "but I know a bunch of people from your organization. Do you know the Townsends? Or Ann Thomas?" Name-dropping would make it seem that I was interested.

"Sure, I know them! In fact I served on a team with Ann," Scott replied.

"Wow! It's such a small world!" I prepared for my exit at this point.

"Are you interested in our summer camp program?"

No, I wanted to say, *I don't want to go to China! China doesn't fit my personality.*

"I don't think I'm interested in a summer program," I said, "but I know you have a year-long tuition-free program. Do you have any information about that?" That would show him he was talking to someone who knew about the organization.

No, I wanted to say, I don't want to go to China! China doesn't fit my personality.

Scott cleared his throat. "I can't really talk about that program. It's by nomination only."

Was he telling me that I, who had prepared for overseas work for years, was not qualified? True, I didn't want to go to China, but to tell me that I *couldn't* go was insulting.

"Oh, really?" I pressed. "And who nominates?"

"Well, the campus pastor or another designee. But it's a very selective program. Not even all of those who are nominated get in. I'm not authorized to talk about that program. I'm sorry," he said, fidgeting with discomfort.

"OK. Thanks. Glad you're here at the conference. Hope it goes well for you," I said.

"You too. Let me know if you ever become interested in the camp program." I shook his hand and walked away.

For the next couple of days, that conversation played over in my head.

I couldn't believe that I—a top student and a seasoned Christian who was interested in overseas work—had been told I didn't qualify for a program. I didn't like crowds, and China has crowds everywhere. I'd never enjoyed any Chinese food I'd tried. And I spoke French and Spanish, not Mandarin or Cantonese. But pride nudged me. I decided to prove that I was good enough to go. I figured I could at least get nominated and then turn down the invitation to join the program.

Sure enough—I talked to the campus pastor, got the nomination, sent in the application, and I was accepted into the program.

Take that, Scott.

Of course during this process my heart and motivations were not in the right place, but God was working on my heart. By the time the acceptance letter came, I was much more interested in going to China—but I faced so many difficulties to work out. What about my education? What would my family say?

What started as an ego-defense mechanism turned into an open door. My university would give me credit for going, and my parents supported the idea. I kept asking God when he would recognize this was all a bluff, but he seemed serious. When decision time arrived, I couldn't find any legitimate reason—other than not being a fan of fish oil—to turn down the opportunity. Soon I was on a plane. I was headed for 11 months in a small, backcountry Chinese village teaching English to middle school and high school students.

The craziest thing of all is that I *loved* China. I even returned for the summer a couple of years later. I loved the people, didn't mind the crowds, enjoyed most of the food, and learned the language.

My times in China were some of the best times of my life. I'm so grateful that I could go. Sometimes people pray for God *not* to send them to a certain mission field; I did the opposite! God could even use my pride to teach me about trusting him to take me where he wants me.

—*Heather Pleier*

WHEN GOD BREAKS THROUGH

Whether we're trying to decide what the future holds or thinking we have life all planned out, it's good to know that God ultimately is in control. When we don't know what the future holds, if we keep obeying God one step at a time, he will lead us to what he has for us. And even if we think we have our plans all figured out, we can still watch God at work through the circumstances in our lives—sometimes confirming our plans, sometimes changing them, sometimes taking us on side trips. God knew you before you were conceived and he knows what will happen every day of your life. The psalmist knew that and rejoiced: "All the days ordained for me were written in your book before one of them came to be. How precious to me are your thoughts, O God! How vast is the sum of them! Were I to count them, they would outnumber the grains of sand. When I awake, I am still with you" (Psalm 139:16–18, NIV).

MY CHALLENGE

Read Psalm 139 aloud. Thank God for his great love for you—he knows everything about you and still loves you. He knows what the future holds, even though you don't. When you're seeking guidance, why not look to the one who already knows your future and wants to walk with you there?

42 A SOLID FOUNDATION?

Preserving a Good Foundation

Those walls look like they might buckle, I thought with a shudder.

The man on the giant yellow backhoe had removed the earth surrounding our house in three big scoops. The gaping chasm revealed the danger that had lurked underground. I surveyed our basement walls and recalled the first clue that something was wrong.

We had hired a contractor to add a second story to our home. "Get the waterproofing done before we start the addition," he said. So I made the call.

"You have big problems, lady," the waterproofer said as he sat at my kitchen table. "You've got serious foundation problems."

I sat there wide-eyed in disbelief. Our basement had never even flooded. What could possibly be so wrong? I insisted on evaluating the situation myself, so I followed the waterproofer to the basement.

As he steadied the red beam of his laser level from one end of a wall to the other, I gasped. Instead of being flat and straight, the walls bowed inward. The upper level of cement blocks had shifted and daylight streamed in through a huge crack. Suddenly I was afraid our house might cave in at any moment.

"What caused the walls to bow?" I demanded.

"Water," he flatly answered.

"This house is 73 years old. Why are we having problems now?"

"Oh, this didn't just happen overnight," he said.

"Can we fix the walls and prevent this from happening again?" I asked.

"It can be fixed, but it ain't gonna be easy or cheap."

Now, for a long time I stood by the trench around my house, staring at the basement walls. How important a good foundation is for a house. *And for life!* I thought.

My foundation is strong, I told myself. I had grown up in a Christian home, had gone to a Christian college, and regularly attended church and a Bible study. I patted myself on the back for building my children's foundation on God and raising them in a Christian home. A certain smugness came over me.

The excavator examined his work and my gaze dropped to the bottom of the trench. Lying on the ground at the base of the wall were pipes—drainage pipes! I peered closer. Could it be? "Well, look at that," the excavator announced. "Drain tile, just like you were going to install."

"You're telling me the answer to our foundation problems was right there all along?" I cried.

"Yep. Your walls wouldn't look like they do if you had a sump pump connected to that drain tile. With no sump pump, those pipes weren't doin' a lick of good."

It all made sense now. I knew our house had been built on a good foundation! If only we had been tied to the drain tile.

Just then I saw God holding a laser level up to my life, and the sight surprised me. Impatience, envy, discontent, and self-absorption stared at me like the cracks in the basement walls. My pride evaporated. Originally my foundation was strong. But every foundation needs to be preserved. My priorities had gotten mixed up and the condition of my life with its pride and self-sufficiency was now exposed like my basement walls. I stood there and asked God's forgiveness.

> *Originally my foundation was strong. But every foundation needs to be preserved.*

I felt grateful to get our home's foundation problems fixed. And I resolved to fix my own personal foundation. I knew what I needed to do—spending time with Jesus had to be my first priority, because a good foundation will not stand without the right connections.

—*Christine Erickson*

ALONG THE WAY

WHEN GOD BREAKS THROUGH

If God held a spiritual laser level to examine your foundation, what would he find? On what is your foundation built? Have you checked it lately? Sometimes we're tempted to coast to complacency, thinking our faith in God will take care of itself. But even the best foundations can develop cracks. Jude 20–21 (NLT) reads, "You, dear friends, build yourselves up in your most holy faith and pray in the Holy Spirit. Keep yourselves in God's love as you wait for the mercy of our Lord Jesus Christ to bring you to eternal life." In other words don't simply have faith in *your faith*. Keep connected to the builder of your foundation—the Lord Jesus—through prayer and by reading the Word.

MY CHALLENGE

Preserving your foundation requires patience and perseverance. Prayerfully consider your foundation. Ask God to help you see the cracks—the blind spots, excuses, and so forth. Allow him to apply his corrective "putty" (forgiveness for a wrong attitude; strength where you're weak). Be open to whatever changes he suggests. Consider also how you can remain connected to the Lord. What changes do you need to make in your routine to develop a stronger connection?

43 IT TAKES A STABLE
Facing Your Fears

Dust covered my clothes and boots. I slumped against the side of my old Jeep parked outside the stables and put my face in my hands. Tears washed the dirt in rivulets down my cheeks as I heard the words echo: "We're letting you go." The therapeutic riding center didn't have the funds to pay me anymore. I thought about the kids who counted on riding the horses each week. What would happen to them now?

I had started at the center as a volunteer. Eventually I earned my certification and became the program director. I loved every minute of working with the children who had various degrees of disability. Joshua, for example, was a whirlwind, but he changed riding the horse. We'd put on his helmet, I'd help him mount, and he'd sit quietly with the volunteer "side walkers" on each side and a leader at the front.

"Are you ready to ride, Joshua?" I'd ask.

"Yes, Miss Darlene."

"Then tell your horse to walk on."

"Walk on," Joshua said confidently.

Joshua learned to follow my directions to turn his horse, stop his horse, and pick up a colored cone from the top of a tall pole.

His mother's eyes widened when she saw this. "I've never seen him sit still for so long!" she exclaimed.

The horse's ears flicked as he listened to Joshua's directives. A horse's kind and gentle nature helps it form a bond with the rider, and riding can help a child physically strengthen muscles while building self-esteem. Joshua didn't know how much this was helping him; he just knew he was having fun.

How can I give this up? I cried as I drove home, plodded into the house, and dropped onto a kitchen chair.

"Honey, they let me go today."

My husband, Bruce, was sorry, but honestly he also was relieved. "You spent too much time at the stables anyway. You neglect our kids."

We'd had this discussion before.

"Get a job where you can spend more time at home with us," he said.

Bruce was right. I often shuttled Kylie and Dane to a sitter. I rationalized that they didn't need the extra attention the children at the riding center required. But was I neglecting them as my husband said?

Starting a center would cost too much money and take too much time.

That night as I got ready for bed, I avoided looking at my dusty boots. I fell into a fitful sleep, and that's when the dream to open my own riding center bubbled inside me.

At first I ignored this thought. Starting a center would cost too much money and take too much time. I would need to put in long hours managing the books, teaching the lessons, and coordinating the volunteers. It was too much to even think about.

I took a job as a teaching assistant at a nearby school. I put on business clothes, drove to the school, and spent the day in a small classroom. I missed the pungent aroma of horses, hay, and my worn-out jeans and clunky boots. I spent more time with Bruce and the kids, but what about the dream God had given me? What about helping kids that too few people helped?

Thoughts about my own center flashed through my mind. If I were ever to do it, I would need clients, saddles, leads, halters, volunteers, and horses. What if I failed? The kids would count on riding. The parents would depend on me. I couldn't stand to disappoint them.

I can't do it by myself, God.

Passing the stables on my drive home from school one day, I saw a girl riding a chestnut mare. With her hair blowing in the breeze and bouncing gently up and down in the saddle as the horse cantered, she looked like a student I used to have—12-year-old Janey, a soft-spoken child with autism. Although Janey was crazy about horses, on first meeting our big chestnut quarter horse, she had refused to even stroke him. By her third lesson, Janey not only petted the horse and held her reins proudly as she sat and waited to ride, she also loudly exclaimed, "Walk on!"

Janey let others help her. And she mastered her fear.

Could I master mine? I sank on to my living room floor and prayed, pouring out all my sorrow at losing my job, all the respect and love I had for my husband even though we didn't always agree, all my fear of starting something so big I knew I couldn't accomplish it alone. I sat there a long time; then I stood up. If kids like Janey could face their fear and trust others to help them, I could too.

I started talking to Bruce. "I don't want to go back to teaching in the fall," I said. I told him all about my dream. My throat tightened and I almost started to cry, but I choked out what I wanted to say. "It means so much to me to work with those kids. I know it will be a lot of work, but I promise to be here as much as I can for you and our kids too."

"If it means that much to you," Bruce said, "let's see if we can work it out." I threw my arms around him.

With Bruce's encouragement I started looking for an arena. That's when I met Cheryl. "Come on, let me show you around," she said when I stopped at the stables. "It's hot and dusty in the summer, and it swamps out when it rains, but it's the perfect size for your needs."

She was right. The arena was perfect. "I don't have horses or tack or well—anything," I stammered.

"I have a horse you can lease to get started," Cheryl offered with a sparkle in her eye. "Don't worry. Everything will work out."

Local businesses donated supplies. I found a deal on saddles, but I still needed volunteers and clients.

I planned a Play Day Horse Show. Friends and family promised to help with the food, the raffle booth, and the riders. But that morning dark clouds rolled in. Rain fell in buckets, splattering mud everywhere. I walked through the drenched arena.

Cheryl was in the front office when I came in, my head hanging low. "Don't worry," she said.

The next morning the phone began to ring. Volunteers asked for the rescheduled date. Three weeks later the Play Day Horse Show turned out great.

The riding program is now running well. We have difficult days, but somehow they all work out. I can't explain it, and I can't control it. Just when I'm ready to freak out, I hear that little voice say, "Uh-uh. This is in my hands, not yours." Whenever I feel that old fear creeping in, I remember the mom who pulled me aside after a lesson. "What you did on the horse today is the most I have seen my daughter respond in four years," she said. "I strongly believe this was what you were meant to do with your life."

So I continue to put my heart and soul into my dream, and God takes care of the rest. It is truly amazing. And so are my relationships with my husband and kids. I don't work as many hours as I used to, and I bring Kylie and Dane to the arena in the summer. They're learning to help others and I'm learning to take a little time for Bruce and me.

God knew my dream was too big for me to achieve alone, and he continues to provide the help I need.

—Darlene H. as told to B. J. Taylor

When God Breaks Through

How often do we dream big dreams, only to stifle our imaginations when the dreams seem too impossible to achieve? Fear can slam the door, even on God-given dreams. What fears do you wrestle? If you feel you're fighting a losing battle, consider this promise from Old Testament prophet Jeremiah: "Blessed are those who trust in the Lord and have made the Lord their hope and confidence" (Jeremiah 17:7, NLT). We often fail to realize the truth of this promise because our confidence lies with our abilities or perspective. Placing our confidence in the Lord lifts the burden of making everything happen ourselves and places it on God, who can make anything happen.

My Challenge

Think about a dream or goal you've had. What fears hinder your meeting this goal or realizing this dream? Write these down. Writing down your fears can give shape to them and help you confront them. Now pray about every fear on your list. Ask God what steps you can take to overcome obstacles. Be open to his suggestions.

Along the Way

44 CLASS REUNION
Seeing God Through Our Friendships

The years seemed to melt away the minute Ann and I met at the airport to attend our first high school reunion together. Although 30 years had passed since graduation, we felt like teenagers as soon as we saw each other. Talk came easily. We drove around town and then strolled over to check out the old library, our church, the Dairy Queen, and our alma mater.

When I knew Ann in high school, her father was an alcoholic, her mother a battered wife. Our gang of friends never went to Ann's house to hang out. There hadn't been anything to envy about Ann's life at all, except that she never had to be home at a certain time and never had to ask permission to go anywhere or do anything. But Ann had eagerly followed Jesus. She turned from the self-destructive blueprint for life provided by her family, married a Christian man, and raised four children for the Lord. All of Ann's children were now raising their children to know and love Jesus.

Walking through the freshly waxed halls of the high school, stepping into classrooms heavy with the scent of old books and whiteboard markers, Ann and I recounted stories from what seemed like the day before. Our laughter echoed down the empty halls, and we half expected a teacher to step out of a classroom and send us to the principal's office.

When we reached the cafeteria, Ann smiled and nudged me. "Remember what happened here?" she asked.

I looked around the room. A dried puddle of soda was under the vending machine. I faintly smelled stale bananas, curdled milk, Italian sausage from Friday's pizza day, and the vat of greasy oil for making french fries. The tables, the posters on the walls—nothing jogged my memory.

"No, but I can't remember much these days," I said with a grin. "What happened here?"

"I can't believe you don't remember!" Ann stared at me in disbelief. "Remember that one day we were about to eat lunch and I asked you what you were doing?"

What did I do 30 years ago in this room that was so earth-shattering?

I sighed with relief. I hadn't forgotten anything big. "Nope. What did I do 30 years ago in this room that was so earth-shattering?" I waited for a remark about some tacky outfit I had worn or a boy who had flirted with me.

"You were praying," Ann said.

I was stunned.

"I thought it such a strange thing to do in front of everyone," Ann continued. "You were so matter-of-fact about it. You invited me to come to church with you the next Sunday. From then on, I went to church with your family during the rest of high school. I became a Christian right here in this room because of you!"

One simple lunch period prayer started a legacy of change.

—*Lori P. as told to Gloria Spielman*

WHEN GOD BREAKS THROUGH

A word of encouragement, a knowing glance, a shared tear. These are ways the Holy Spirit unites believers to one another and draws us to himself. We can know we have encountered him when we experience joy, healing, bonds of friendship, and loving encouragement through other believers. That is God in our midst.

MY CHALLENGE

Read Paul's words to his dear brothers and sisters at Thessalonica, "As for us, we always thank God for you, dear brothers and sisters loved by the Lord. We are thankful that God chose you to be among the first to experience salvation, a salvation that came through the Spirit who makes you holy and by your belief in the truth. He called you to salvation when we told you the Good News; now you can share in the glory of our Lord Jesus Christ" (2 Thessalonians 2:13–14, NLT). Whom has God brought into your life to help you and encourage your faith? Tell God how thankful you are for those people and pray for them. And if you haven't told those friends how they have influenced you, do so this week.

45 TROUBLED WATERS

Experiencing Jesus in Life's Emergencies

"Dad! Dad!"

Somehow I heard my five-year-old son David's frantic voice above my portable radio and the ocean breakers crashing along the African shoreline. I pulled the headphones off my ears.

"Dad! A big wave came in and pulled Matthew out to sea!" David cried.

I sprinted down the beach, cold fear propelling my feet.

As a missionary in West Africa, I loved bringing my family to this remote vacation spot on the tropical ocean every year. I knew the waters before me were deceptively treacherous. The sea appeared smooth and calm, sunlight sparkling off the temperate water. But just when one might have relaxed, enormous waves rolled in, flooding the beach. And when they receded, they dragged everything in their wake back out to sea.

And this time they had dragged my son with them.

There, bobbing high on a dark, choppy wave about 30 yards out, was my youngest son. He looked at me as the undertow pulled him farther away from the shore. I hit the water.

Oh, Jesus, help me, please!

I swam as fast as I could toward four-year-old Matt, keeping my eyes riveted on his. If he went under that dark, swirling mass of water, I would never find him again.

177

I passed my six-year-old, Malcolm, who was trying to fight the waves to get to Matt. "Go back to shore!" I yelled. "I'll get him!"

The water was roiling; I now understood why some Africans thought of the ocean as a great, dark, angry power. Matt floated on the surface, never taking his eyes off me as I approached.

Finally our bodies touched in the cold water. Nothing has ever felt so wonderfully secure as my son's small body wrapping around my arm and shoulder. I turned and began to pull the two of us against the ocean's thrust, exerting all my effort to fight against that riptide. As I headed toward shore, my fear slowly subsided. The sandy yellow shoreline had never looked so beautiful!

He looked at me as the undertow pulled him farther away from the shore. I hit the water.

When we reached Malcolm, now trying to go inland against the still-powerful undertow, he climbed "on board" as well, and the three of us progressed to shallow water where we could finally put our feet on the sandy bottom and stumbled the last few yards to the beach.

We fell to the hot sand, exhausted.

Matt sat up and grinned. "I knew you would come and get me," he said. "I wasn't even afraid."

My son's faith in me was stronger than my faith in God had been; I had been terrified as I entered the cold ocean.

I looked at my son, his hair sticking up in the middle, and thought of Jesus' words, "Are not five sparrows sold for two pennies? Yet not one of them is forgotten by God. Indeed, the very hairs of your head are all numbered. Don't be afraid; you are worth more than many sparrows" (Luke 12:6–7, NIV).

Jesus, thank you! My sons mean more to you than they do even to me, although I cannot imagine that.

Sometimes, now that my boys have grown into strong young men, I wonder what purposes God has for their lives. It must be something important, because Jesus himself was with us that day. I don't know any lifesaving techniques nor am I a particularly strong swimmer. How else could I have made it back to shore against that murderous undertow with two boys in my arms?

It could have only been God—proving his faithfulness and might and love for us, even against the odds of treacherous waters.

—Gene Smillie

WHEN GOD BREAKS THROUGH

Before Jesus returned to his heavenly home, he left his disciples with a powerful promise: "And be sure of this: I am with you always, even to the end of the age" (Matthew 28:20, NLT). Jesus is not only with us on terrible days, but on every day. That's what he promised. We don't always see Jesus or sense him. But we experience moments when, if he were not there with us, we know our lives and situations would have turned out far differently than they did.

MY CHALLENGE

When have you experienced Jesus' presence? How can you become more conscious of ways he is with you through the day? Consider ways Jesus was with you the past 24 hours.

ALONG THE WAY

46 FREE TO RECEIVE
Understanding God's Faithfulness

"Can you believe it? We're actually moving to Colorado, Andy!"

My husband and I sat outside our favorite ice cream store, slurping smoothies before we pulled away from the familiar streets of Hillsdale, Michigan. Earlier in the day we'd loaded the moving truck, given our final hugs, cranked up the air conditioning, and waved goodbye to friends and family.

We couldn't stop smiling. It was bold. It was thrilling! We'd been planning this move for six months. I had to keep reminding myself that today it was actually happening, almost like the day we were married. But instead of "We just got married!" it was "We're moving to Colorado!"

As we drove the massive yellow truck across the country with our car in tow, we prayed, talked, laughed, sat silently, and took turns feeling the baby kick inside me. I was in someone else's romantic comedy/adventure movie—and I was loving every moment!

A longtime friend had invited us to help plant a new church in Boulder. We would meet the rest of the ministry team when we arrived. The hours on the road were long, but every hour took us closer to our new church community.

We finally pulled up in front of the home of Brady and Julie Smith late one evening. We were thrilled to finally meet them. We had corresponded only through e-mail. Brady had introduced himself and offered their home as a place for us to start because they had an extra bedroom and bathroom. After we accepted his invitation, Brady sent us $500 to help with moving expenses. We were a bit taken aback by the gift; we had never encountered this type of generosity before—and certainly not from people we'd never really met.

The Smiths' openhanded way of living left its mark on us during the month we stayed with them. We repeatedly watched them give their time and resources to us and to others in the community. We hoped to be like them someday.

But at that time we were focused on our own needs. Our first several months in Boulder were hard. Very hard. Andy was unable to find work right away, and we did not have

Had we made a mistake? . . . Why did I feel so abandoned?

medical care ready for the baby. I began to doubt our move, and in my mind I could hear friends and family back home saying, "The three biggest stresses on a marriage are moving, changing jobs, and having a baby. And you're doing all three at once!"

Were they right? Had we made a mistake? I thought we were doing what God wanted by moving across the country to join a promising new ministry. Why did I feel so abandoned?

In frustration and desperation I sought the Lord by praying, reading Scripture, and writing in my journal. Andy and I spent a lot of time praying together as well. God kept pointing us toward accounts of his faithfulness, telling us to take him at his word. And while we were learning these things, he continued to provide for us, giving us just what we needed when we needed it.

We received checks in the mail, encouraging e-mails from friends back home, and increasing financial assistance from our new church community. We were given meals and a car to borrow when ours broke down. Rent

181

money for our apartment arrived just before it was due. I found a doctor for the baby right before the time for my next checkup. Dollars stretched in ways I had never seen before.

Not being in control drove me crazy, and it drove me to the arms of my Savior.

When I looked past the details of our situation and stopped comparing our finances to others around us, I no longer felt so far away from God. He was right here in our midst, taking care of us through others. Jesus was present and was faithful through his body, the church.

We've been in Boulder for more than a year now, and our lives are more stable. Little Mercy is 10 months old. We're settled into our neighborhood. Paychecks are more regular. But our hearts are still tender because of what happened last summer. We don't want to bounce back to our old do-it-yourself lifestyle. We keep running to God.

—Betsy Zenz

When God Breaks Through

"Great is his faithfulness; his mercies begin afresh each day" (Lamentations 3:23, NLT). Betsy learned firsthand what it meant to watch for God's faithfulness and grace each and every day. During those first difficult up-in-the-air months in Colorado, she watched God constantly provide for their needs. And how appropriate that as Andy and Betsy came to minister and help build a church, they were being taught an invaluable lesson about what the church really is. It is not a building or a program; it is a group of believers who seek to know God and live life as he teaches us to. Jesus allowed Betsy and her husband to need him in new ways. As they saw his faithfulness and mercies each day, those lessons stayed with them. They saw God's blessings in their lives and were set free to let those blessings overflow into the lives around them.

My Challenge

Take a moment to reflect on the various ways that God has shown himself to you. When you look closely, you too will begin to see God's faithfulness and grace afresh each day. Ask God to show himself to you today. And then watch what happens!

ALONG THE WAY

47 TRANSFORMED BY LOVE
Discovering the Power of God's Great Love

More than anything else in the world, I wanted a hug and kiss from our son, Sam. We adopted Sam from China when he was not quite two years old, and he had no interest in cuddling, giving kisses, or any other kind of touch.

My husband, Tim, and I learned about Sam three months after we returned home from China with our first adopted child, Anna. Tim had noticed that our adoption agency had a new Waiting Children list on its website and told me about it. All the little ones on the list had special needs. He has always had a special place in his heart for children.

Later that evening I told Tim I had looked at the list and noticed a little boy the agency dubbed James, who had been born with a severe bilateral cleft lip and palate. Tim had been thinking about the same boy! But having just adopted Anna, we had no more money in savings and knew we couldn't adopt another child right then. James was the youngest on the list, only ten months old, so we were sure he would be adopted soon. We checked the agency's website every day to see if he had been chosen yet. But he remained on the list.

A few months later we received a card from a relative that included a check for us to spend however we wanted. We looked at each other, both thinking the same thing—*James*. We called our agency, and they had just returned James' file to the sponsoring organization. Fortunately, they got it back for us.

As our paper chase began, we wondered where the rest of the money would come from. As we prayed and continued to move forward in faith, we began to see the funding come in. Extra work, a bigger tax refund than expected, and another unexpected gift. We knew this child was meant to be our son.

We put ourselves on a strict budget, and by the time our travel dates arrived, we had the money we needed—and even some extra in savings. We packed our bags, did our best to prepare Anna

What if he didn't like us? What if he and Anna didn't get along?

for a new brother (who was only three weeks younger), gave James his new name—Sam—and started thinking about how life would be when we got him home. We had adopted Anna at seven months, and she had bonded with us and adjusted to her new life fairly quickly. But Sam was older. What if he didn't like us? What if he and Anna didn't get along? What if he had attachment issues?

When we saw Sam we fell even more deeply in love with him. Despite his facial deformities, his wide smile was gorgeous, and his brown eyes danced. But in the process of going home, those eyes also held fear. Sam was traumatized. Besides his adjustment to a new language, new food, and new faces, Sam endured three surgeries and four hospitalizations that changed the anatomy of his mouth and nose. He faced speech and occupational therapy sessions too. That's a lot for one little boy to go through in a year. He was easily frustrated over everything. He cried a lot, and clung to me for dear life. I think I carried him for the entire first year he was home.

After that first year, little by little, we saw changes in Sam. He was learning to use words instead of communicating with grunts and screams. He learned to feed himself, drink from a cup, and be more patient. And then he began letting me hug and kiss him. Slowly but surely we began to see a new boy emerge—happy-go-lucky, comfortable, fun, and loving.

One night as I put Sam to bed, I told him a story and sang his favorite song, "'Tis So Sweet to Trust in Jesus." From the first time I sang it to him in China, the song had always soothed him.

As we rested there Sam gently cupped my face with his little hands and said softly, "I love you, Mommy." And then he laid a sweet little kiss on my nose. I'll never forget that moment.

In the three years Sam has been with us, he has endured four more surgeries and continues to struggle with speech. The physical differences in Sam are astounding, but the changes in his spirit and countenance are even greater. Sam is a changed boy. Once he was scared; now he trusts. Once he was traumatized; now he is joyful. Once he avoided affection and closeness; now he doles out hugs and kisses to our family. Every night when I put him to bed he says, "I love you" to all of us. Sam has been transformed by love.

—*Alison Simpson*

WHEN GOD BREAKS THROUGH

Your love, O LORD, reaches to the heavens, your faithfulness to the skies. Your righteousness is like the mighty mountains, your justice like the great deep. O LORD, you preserve both man and beast. How priceless is your unfailing love! Both high and low among men find refuge in the shadow of your wings. They feast on the abundance of your house; you give them drink from your river of delights. For with you is the fountain of life; in your light we see light (Psalm 36:5–9, NIV).

Little Sam received love from his new family and was changed by it. From a scared little boy to a loving son, Sam was changed from the inside out. Isn't that what happens to all of us when we encounter God's love? Once we were lost in sin, separated from God, without hope. But then God finds us and brings us into his family. His love and forgiveness change us. We become different people when we let his love into our lives. God says, "I love you, no matter what!" No matter how much you were broken, hurting, or deprived of nurturing, God can transform you. His love reaches to the heavens!

MY CHALLENGE

How has God's love for you made a difference in your life? Look up these other verses about God's great love for you: Psalm 25:6–7; John 3:16; Romans 8:28–39; Ephesians 3:16–21; 1 John 3:16; 4:19.

ALONG THE WAY

48 STANDING GUARD
Discerning God's Protection

The children and I snuggled on the couch, reading aloud from C. S. Lewis' *The Horse and His Boy*, when a dog began barking outside, harsh and angry and loud.

We didn't own a dog. Neighborhood dogs barked, of course, but always at a distance, their yaps and howls filtering faintly through the oak and hemlock trees surrounding our home. This barking, however, was distinct and close. Some dog, from somewhere, had planted itself in front of our house and was barking at us. Or at something he saw.

Our house had no windows on the side where we were sitting, and with my husband out of town, I refused to open the door and lose its protection against danger. I laid down the book and toured the house with my two children, trying to make a game of checking the bedrooms, the kitchen, and then the downstairs entry. We saw nothing unusual inside the house or through the windows in those rooms. We circled back to the couch. I picked up the book and read to the end of the chapter, sometimes nearly shouting to be heard above the dog's continued barking. Then we prayed, and I tucked each child into bed.

Once both children were cuddled under their comforters, I willed myself to explore the house again. I checked each door lock and peered through each window, looking for an answer to the puzzle. With each of the dog's staccato barks, my muscles knotted tighter. Did he see something that I should be guarding against? Was a prowler, hidden by darkness, searching for a way to enter my home? Did I need help?

I thought of telephoning someone, but we were new to the neighborhood and I didn't know my neighbors' names well enough to find their numbers in the phone book. I could have called someone farther away—or even the police—but I thought I would sound ridiculous: "Could you please come to my house because I'm frightened by a barking dog?"

I returned to the couch, turned off the lights, and sat as though frozen. I listened to the dog's labored breaths between each burst of barking, feeling as though the wall between us had worn so thin that I could touch him.

I knelt beside the couch and prayed. "Protect us please, God. Circle us with guardians." I thought of the children in their beds. "Keep us safe."

I got up when my daughter called. "Mommy, what if the dog sees something bad and is trying to warn us?"

"God is big, you know that," I said. I sat down on Connie's bed and rubbed my hand over her forehead and hair. "Anything that's out there, well even if it's big, God's bigger. He knows more, sees more, and hears more than we do. He can take care of us."

With each of the dog's staccato barks, my muscles knotted tighter. Did he see something that I should be guarding against?

Peter stumbled in from his room, sat on the carpet, and leaned against me. I told them the Old Testament story of the prophet Elisha's servant, who was terribly scared when he got out of his sleeping bag one morning and saw enemy soldiers surrounding their camp. But God let the servant see what we usually can't see: what the servant thought was an empty field actually swarmed with God's own bodyguards. Horses and chariots of fire surrounded them, ready to protect the servants of God from their enemies.

I tucked both children into bed and tiptoed back to the living room.

I didn't feel nearly as confident as I had sounded, but I knew that if God wanted to protect us, he would find a way.

By now the dog had been barking for almost thirty minutes. Then I remembered, we had recently installed a motion light on the other side of the house. I calmed myself and relaxed into the couch cushions. If someone were prowling around the house, I reasoned, the light would have been triggered. I had no reason to be anxious unless the light turned on.

The light turned on.

I learned then that fear has a taste. My mouth went dry; my stomach turned sour. My ears pulsed with the sound of each heartbeat.

A fist banged hard on the door downstairs.

"God, help me." I switched off the light and carefully negotiated the stairs in the dark. If I had to go down there, I didn't want this person to see me through a window before I saw him.

More thuds sounded against the wooden door.

As I walked toward the door, I peered at the closed curtains on either side of the entryway. I could see a silhouette. I held my breath, reached forward, slid the curtain to the side—and looked out. A man stood outside my door, the motion light casting him in shadow. It took me several seconds to recognize the hard-brimmed hat, square shoulders, and upright posture of a state trooper.

My relief was palpable. I unlocked and opened the door. Only then was I aware that the dog had stopped barking.

"Do you live in this house?" the trooper began, startling me with the question as soon as I opened the door.

My tongue felt heavy and dry. I couldn't seem to make it move.

"Have you heard a dog barking?" he asked.

During the moment it took me to respond, I turned on the overhead light. The officer looked at me closely. Once he saw me in the light, his tone changed.

"Are you frightened?" he asked.

"Not . . . anymore," I stammered.

"A neighbor—I don't know who—called us. They thought maybe you had an emergency here."

Satisfied I was safe, the trooper said good night and walked away, shining his flashlight along the uphill side of the house, along the path, and beyond as he walked toward his car. As he backed out of our driveway, I watched him slowly rake the woods with the cruiser's spotlight.

Days later when I finished reading *The Horse and His Boy* aloud, Connie and Peter pointed out that Aslan, the lion king in the story, had been watching over the boy, Shasta, even when Shasta didn't recognize him. We knew that God was also looking out for us on that frightening night.

Whenever fear threatens to overpower me, I remember that night when God used a loud dog, an anonymous neighbor, and a state trooper to watch over us. While fear might be capable of overwhelming me, it can't overwhelm God. "Cast all your anxiety upon him because he cares for you" (1 Peter 5:7, NIV).

—Martha Manikas-Foster

WHEN GOD BREAKS THROUGH

When we're in the midst of a fearful situation like Martha's, we can't always see past the circumstance. Yet God is with us all the time, though his methods are often too cloaked for us to see. Sometimes, like Elijah's servant, we get a glimpse.

> When the servant of the man of God got up and went out early the next morning, an army with horses and chariots had surrounded the city. "Oh, my lord, what shall we do?" the servant asked. "Don't be afraid," the prophet answered. "Those who are with us are more than those who are with them."
>
> And Elisha prayed, "O LORD, open his eyes so he may see." Then the LORD opened the servant's eyes, and he looked and saw the hills full of horses and chariots of fire all around Elisha.—2 Kings 6:15–17, NIV

Fear pushes the panic button within us. Sometimes we're so paralyzed by fear that we don't think to call out. Or we might think we won't be heard if we make the effort. That's why prayer is a necessary part of any emergency preparedness regimen. If we get into the habit of praying, it will be second nature when an emergency arises. The great thing about God is that he can arrive on the scene far quicker than any emergency worker!

MY CHALLENGE

You probably have phone numbers to call (police, fire, your doctor, a family member, or close friend) in case of emergency. Make a list of God's promises to use when you're feeling challenged or fearful. Consider the above passage from 2 Kings and passages such as Joshua 1:5–9; Psalm 23:4; 40:1–3; 116:6.

49 ONE WAY TO AMERICA, PLEASE

Learning to Wait as God Works Behind the Scenes

"Daniela, you need to sit down," my husband said to me from the other end of the phone line. He was calling from work, and my heart began to pound as I thought of his possible news. Five years earlier, when we arrived in Richmond after a stressful job search, my husband's employer had announced a large "redeployment." Was it happening again?

I asked in a quiet voice, "Have you lost your job, Daniel?"

Only silence came over the line.

SWITZERLAND TO MIAMI, ONE WAY read our airplane tickets as we departed our homeland in 1998 to begin my husband's MBA program at the University of Miami. Little did we know that the easiest part of the journey was packing a container with our family's belongings and leaving our home country.

For more than a decade before that, Daniel and I traveled the world, working in countries such as China and South Africa. In the end we fell in love with America and its citizens and wanted to settle here. After completing his MBA, Daniel began the search for an employer to sponsor us so we could obtain a green card that would allow us to stay in the country. We encountered our first roadblock early on when Daniel couldn't find a job in Florida because he didn't speak fluent Spanish. He spoke English, Swiss, and German, yes, but not Spanish!

At the time I met weekly with a Bible study group and asked them to pray about the situation. God answered within two days when Daniel received an offer to work in Virginia at a bank. After the required performance period ended, the bank started the sponsorship process for our permanent residency. We seemed to be on our way to citizenship.

September 11, 2001, changed the world in many ways. For those seeking to become American citizens, like us, the tragedy complicated the application process by bogging down the system with stricter immigration laws. We found ourselves in a struggle beyond our control.

Then the bank announced the "redeployments." I went into a panic. The sponsorship process forbade him to change jobs, even within the company itself. If Daniel lost his job, we would have to return immediately to Switzerland. We had worked outside Switzerland for so many years that returning there and paying into its social security system was a daunting challenge. To further complicate matters, our son Steven, born in New Jersey, saw himself as an American who loved the United States. He didn't want to leave his country.

The burden for citizenship seemed to be on Daniel's shoulders, but I wanted to help somehow. If I found a job in the U.S., we'd have a backup plan if Daniel lost his job. I had been trained as a practical nurse in Switzerland, but the Board of Nursing didn't recognize my Swiss degree. I decided to start from scratch and earn a bachelor's degree in nursing. I had no desire to return to school, but at least my student status would allow us to stay in the country on a student visa. I planned every detail without praying about it.

My strategies became more and more complicated. To get into a nursing program, I needed to take courses in social studies and English composition and take the SATs before applying to nursing school. Seeing no other option, I attended classes at the local community college. I fulfilled all the requirements and filed my application, only to be rejected by the nursing program. The long, complicated process had not paid off, except for one benefit: I became friends with my English composition professor who happened to be a Christian. We kept in touch, and she invited me to be a part of her women's Bible study group.

Every time our group met, I asked them to pray about our immigration ordeal. The law only allowed six years to complete the green card process. At the end of those six years, we needed to reapply for the visa, starting the long process all over again. Often I felt panicky about how our file seemed to get lost in that process.

One morning after reading a devotional, I asked myself if I really prayed with faith believing God would answer. For the first time I saw that I hadn't handed the problem over to him. Instead I had been working on my own solution, trying to make it happen.

We needed a miracle. Time was running out.

The next time our ladies group met, I confessed my lack of faith. After that my prayers changed because I knew we had God fighting for us! I had always known in the past that God fought for me and other believers, but that faith seemed hidden behind a veil, filled with questioning and doubts. Suddenly the veil was removed, replaced by an assurance that we would be able to stay in the country.

Along with my newfound faith, more roadblocks appeared. The immigration lawyer told us our file was backlogged with many other applications. It could take months or even years to get caught up. I asked my friends again to pray that our file would be pulled from the stack. We needed a miracle. Time was running out.

A short time later we received a phone call from the immigration office.

They needed copies of our important paperwork—birth certificates, marriage license, and so forth— because someone pulled our file and began working on it again! After we provided the requested materials, we were told we might have a 12- to 36-month wait until we received our green cards.

They gave us an I.D. number to monitor our file's progress on the immigration website. We checked the status often. Our file vanished from the computer system. The situation puzzled even the immigration lawyers. Through it all though, I had learned to trust Jesus. I just prayed and stopped checking the website. Suddenly one day our file appeared back in the system!

Now I waited for Daniel to speak. After a long pause on the phone, he blurted out, "We got the green card approval!"

Technically it should have taken another year to get to our file, but God intervened. "This is a miracle!" I said. I hung up the phone and fell on my knees in tears, thanking God for his incredible help.

Less than two weeks later, we held the two green cards in our hands. Today I see that every aspect of the experience was part of God's plan: every friend, every prayer, every block in our path. Most of all, I learned not to face life alone. Jesus proved he meant what he said, "Give it all to me!"

—Daniela R. as told to Linda MacKillop

WHEN GOD BREAKS THROUGH

There are two contrasting ideas about waiting in Scripture. In Psalm 27:14, we wait on God: "Wait for the LORD; be strong and take heart and wait for the LORD" (NIV). But Isaiah 30:18 (NKJV) shows that God also waits for us: "Therefore the LORD will wait, that He may be gracious to you; and therefore He will be exalted, that He may have mercy on you." But in either case, the ball is in God's court.

Waiting isn't passive, however. It is an act of trust—a loving agreement between two parties. You trust that God will act out of his love for you.

MY CHALLENGE

Perhaps there is an answer to prayer for which you've waited for a long time. Are you willing to persist in waiting, even if you don't yet see an answer? Talk with God about what waiting means for you. You might make an agreement with God, telling him that you're committed to waiting on his timing.

ALONG THE WAY

50 A Doubter's Prayer

Meeting God Through Uncertainties

As I sat in the doctor's office for a routine physical, I recounted months of misery. I was dealing with yet another sinus infection and ear infection and was tired of carrying boxes of tissues wherever I went. I told the doctor that I'd experienced incidents of my heart racing, that I'd been losing hair, that I'd lost 30 pounds, and that I was tired all the time. I figured those symptoms were just from stress. The sinus and ear infections were my real concern. I was convinced I needed to see an ear, nose, and throat specialist.

"Have you noticed the large lump on your neck?" the doctor asked.

Part of my brain heard her question, but my mind was focused on getting a referral to see an ENT specialist.

"Now about the referral. This congestion is terrible," I pushed.

"I think you may have an enlarged thyroid gland," the doctor continued, refusing to be pushed off track herself. "We need to have that looked at. It's called a goiter."

"Fine. But could you give me a referral for this constant congestion?"

"I'm going to order a thyroid ultrasound."

"OK. But can you refer me to an ENT too?"

I finally got my referral and felt satisfied. Nothing like setting out to do something and actually getting it done.

The ENT recommended surgery for a blocked sinus cavity. "November 3 is the earliest we can do it," the scheduling clerk told me as she jotted down my name. That was three months away. I took out my pocket calendar and wrote it in. I felt a sense of control.

The endocrinologist, however, had more bad news.

"You have a goiter. Your blood work shows that you have a condition called Grave's disease. That explains some of your symptoms—rapid heart rate, hair loss, fatigue."

Now I was worried.

What is this? Grave's disease? That doesn't sound good, I ruminated. I was losing control. *What is going on? Help me, Lord.*

"Let's start by getting your thyroid levels back to normal with medication," the doctor said, "and then we'll discuss the next step."

With the help of one of those jumbo pill organizers—seven plastic compartments with lids labeled for each day of the week: S, M, T, W, T, F, S—I quickly got used to the daily routine of morning and afternoon pills, nine pills

What is this? Grave's disease? That doesn't sound good . . .

every day. Counting my pills into the container each week helped me regain a sense of control and calm in my life. I could handle this.

Then one morning my husband made a suggestion that completely threw me off kilter. "One of the visiting pastors will pray over people for healing tomorrow morning. You should go."

I was flooded with doubt.

Hadn't I already been asking God to help me? I reasoned. *Besides, God doesn't heal people today, does he? Would God heal someone with such little faith?*

In spite of my skepticism, the next morning I sat on a bench outside the sanctuary, sheepishly waiting for my turn to see the visiting pastor. "Lord, help my unbelief," I murmured as I walked toward the pastor, my knees shaking with doubt. *Will the pastor know I have doubts? Can he tell I'm not sure I believe God* can *heal me? Maybe I shouldn't have come.*

The pastor gently touched my sinuses and my neck and prayed for healing. It wasn't weird; it wasn't scary. And at that moment I knew God was telling me to come to him as a little child and ask.

I began to cry as I prayed, *I'm giving it all up to you, God—the sickness, my attempts to control, my preconceived notions of who you are and what you do. If you want to heal me, I know you can.*

One year later I am off all medications. The sinus surgery was canceled, and my thyroid returned to normal. I am healthier now than I have been in 10 years. I thank God daily for how he delivered me in more ways than I could imagine.

And once a month, a group of people from my church gathers to pray for those who are sick. We don't presume to know God's timing or how he will heal—miraculously or through medical treatments—but we pray, believing that he can heal and that our prayers make a difference.

Now as I go through my day and pray, "Lord, help me," those are not the empty words they used to be. Whenever I look at my kitchen window, I see a jumbo pill organizer sitting on the sill—empty—a daily reminder of God's care for me.

—*Crista V. Forstrom*

When God Breaks Through

In Mark 9:14–24 (NLT) an anguished father asked Jesus to remove the evil spirit from his son. "Do something if you can," the father begged of Jesus.

And Jesus' reply? "What do you mean, 'If I can?' Anything is possible if a person believes." The father instantly countered, "Help me not to doubt."

We all have times in our lives when we need help not to doubt. Will God heal our child? Can God take care of our ailing parent? Will God provide what we need?

We cannot attain this attitude of confidence that we call faith without help. It is a gift from God. It's not something we can store away to use when life gets tough. It's not something we obtain so we can be self-sufficient. Rather, growing in faith is a process of daily trusting in Jesus and depending upon him.

My Challenge

Write down the situation in which you need God's gift of faith today. Ask God to give you the faith you need for this. As part of your prayer, say aloud these words from Psalm 116: "I love the Lord because he hears and answers my prayers. Because he bends down and listens, I will pray as long as I have breath" (Psalm 116:1–2, NLT).

51 THE WRITING ON THE WALL

Remembering God's Constant Presence

GOD IS HERE.

As I stared at the words that morning, I realized I'd never expected God to minister to my heart through graffiti.

I'd first noticed the graffiti a few weeks earlier. As a young minister to a growing congregation, I needed time to myself. Then I discovered a quiet spot underneath the stairway that led to the second-floor sanctuary. It was away from the office and few people passed through this nook.

Light from a nearby window bathed the area, which had a bench and stored lost items—Bibles, Sunday school materials, coats. The spot was partially enclosed, a good hiding place for seasonal decorations and silk flower arrangements. A good hiding place for me too. With Bible in hand, I could read Scripture, pray, and meditate. It was a perfect escape.

One day when I arrived at my hidden prayer closet, I stretched my legs across the bench and leaned against the wall. Looking up, I noticed three words etched in the brown steel frame of the stairs: *GOD WAS HERE.*

I did a double take. Then I chuckled as I realized one of our creative teenagers had probably carved the words while playing hide-and-seek at an all-night lock-in. As I continued my quiet time, I pondered those words with a new perspective that just as God had been on Mount Sinai with

Moses, on Mount Carmel with Elijah, and at Moriah with Abraham, he had been underneath the stairwell of Emmanuel Baptist Church in Overland Park, Kansas. I walked away from my meditation time with a renewed sense of God's presence.

Later that week, just as my wife and I drifted to sleep one night, I received a call from the pastor of my parents' church in Alabama.

"Rick, I have some bad news," he began. "Your father has had a heart attack."

"How is he?"

The pastor paused. "Rick, he passed away."

I was stunned as I listened to the details. Daddy had been sitting on the family room sofa with my mother and my oldest sister when he gasped for air and collapsed, lifeless.

I was 26, married less than a year, and had just begun my first full-time job after years of school. Daddy had always been a confidant, an encourager, a supporter, and a source of wisdom and guidance. I needed him during this season of my life. Suddenly he was gone.

The next day my wife and I drove for 12 hours to Alabama. I kept hoping that it was just a bad dream. But it was not a dream. It was real. A few days later we buried Daddy, and two weeks later we left my mother in Alabama and drove home to Kansas.

I knew Daddy had lived a full life in his 72 years. He had touched many people. So many folks came to his funeral and told wonderful stories and memories about him. But I still felt so alone.

After a few days back in the office at church, I returned to my quiet place under the stairs. I needed peace from the frustrations of a crowded day. I was missing my daddy. Loneliness gripped my heart. I cleared off the bench, sat down, propped my feet up, leaned back, and looked up. The three words were still there, but something was different. They had been tampered with. Altering graffiti on the stairwell of a church? But yes, there was a change. And better yet, my seminary training confirmed that the statement was now more theologically accurate. Someone had crossed through the word WAS and written above it IS.

In that secluded spot a sermon of comfort was preached: GOD IS HERE. Sitting alone there in my stairwell retreat, I knew I would not have Daddy with me on this earth again, but I would always have the Lord. I remembered the promise God gave to Moses: "My Presence will go with you, and I will give you rest" (Exodus 33:14, NIV).

In that secluded spot a sermon of comfort was preached: GOD IS HERE.

I miss my daddy. Nearly every day I think of him and recall something he did or said. One of Daddy's abiding traits was his involvement in my life—and he consistently pointed me to my heavenly Father who will always be there for me.

Whenever I need to be reminded of that, I think of the three words of graffiti I found in my stairwell retreat.

—Rick Ezell

WHEN GOD BREAKS THROUGH

Often when tragedy interrupts our lives, we ask God, "Why?" But God rarely gives an answer or advice. Instead he does something better. He wraps us in his arms and gives us himself. If you are facing a loss—a parent's death, a rebellious child, a child moving to college, or another tough life change—remember that God may not offer you an explanation or resolve your situation. But he will take you in his arms. He holds you and lets you know that you are loved. Don't just seek answers to your troubling questions—look for the God who is trying to break through to embrace you, his child.

MY CHALLENGE

The Lord himself goes before you and will be with you; he will never leave you nor forsake you. Do not be afraid; do not be discouraged (Deuteronomy 31:8, NIV).

The eternal God is your refuge, and his everlasting arms are under you (Deuteronomy 33:27, NLT).

Take a few moments to reflect on these two verses. When have you felt God's everlasting arms underneath you? How have you felt the comfort of God's presence in your current situation?

✤
---

52 A SPECIAL GIRL
Praying for God to Work in Someone's Life

Green dress . . . tulle skirt with daisies scattered in random fashion . . . brown sandals . . . hair in five or six ponytails . . . a beautiful, silly smile. This was the picture I saw on an adoption agency's website—a nine-year-old girl with vision issues.

A girl who would never be my daughter.

Many agencies that handle international adoptions have "waiting children" lists that include orphans with special needs who require loving homes. These children have challenges such as cleft palates, missing limbs, deafness, blindness, and albinism.

Three years ago my husband and I adopted a boy with cleft lip and palate from one of these lists. I continued to casually glance at the lists just to see if the children were being adopted. As an adoptive parent I felt great joy when children found their forever families. I also tended to live vicariously through people who were adopting again. We knew we couldn't adopt again for a long time. Our lives were full with two preschoolers, one with significant medical needs. We just couldn't financially swing another adoption. It was not an option for us.

But for some reason when I saw this little girl's picture, I felt drawn to her in a way that I've never felt while looking at these lists—except when

LONG THE WAY

we first saw our son on a similar list. I could not get her off my mind. So I mentioned it to my husband who has an equally mushy heart when it comes to waiting children. He agreed that she was definitely wonderful. But he said, "Honey, we just have no money."

He was right. Even if we tried to adopt her, we didn't look good enough on paper to be approved for adoption.

I checked the website every day to see if she was still available. Every day she was still unclaimed. It's always sad to see a special-needs child's files sent back to his or her country. But for some reason, the thought of this little Chinese girl not being adopted just tore at me. What could I do? I kept going back to the money issue. We just didn't have it. So what was this tug at my heart?

This was the picture I saw on an adoption agency's website . . .

A girl who would never be my daughter.

I decided to pray. Maybe my prayers were needed to move my husband's heart and change our finances. Maybe I needed to have faith that God could make the impossible possible. So I prayed that if we were being called to step forward as her parents, God would provide the money and also call my husband to it. But neither of those things happened. Over time instead of praying that I would be her mother, I started praying that God would find someone to adopt her and give her a warm home and a loving family.

A few weeks later I heard the happy news: One of the agency's clients decided to adopt her. The little girl will probably come home next spring to live with a sister and a brother who also were adopted from China. Her adoptive mother is excited about becoming this special girl's mother.

While I'm not a part of that family, I feel as if that little girl is a part of me because she taught me something about God. For the first time I learned that God specifically asks us to pray for something even when we are not a part of the answer. That was my role in this special girl's life.

—*Alison Simpson*

WHEN GOD BREAKS THROUGH

Sometimes the best answer to a need isn't our direct involvement in someone's life, but a behind-the-scenes approach through prayer. The Apostle Paul knew this. Although he had the worn sandals of a well-traveled missionary, he couldn't be everywhere at once. So he wrote letters to encourage the members of the churches he planted. He began many letters with a reminder that he was praying for the believers.

> We have not stopped praying for you since we first heard about you. We ask God to give you complete knowledge of his will and to give you spiritual wisdom and understanding. Then the way you live will always honor and please the Lord, and your lives will produce every kind of good fruit. All the while, you will grow as you learn to know God better and better. We also pray that you will be strengthened with all his glorious power so you will have all the endurance and patience you need (Colossians 1:9–12, NLT).

We can't always be with someone or meet their needs directly. But God, who is everywhere all at once, can.

MY CHALLENGE

Make a list of the people and needs that come to mind. If you can't think of a need, consider praying for each person according to Paul's prayer in Colossians 1:9–12.

53 MORE THAN WORDS CAN SAY

Loving for the Long Haul

I had known Jay for years, but that morning when he called me—the first time Jay had ever called me—I knew the news wasn't going to be good. The police had paid a visit to his house the night before. Their report had crushed his mom. His father, several years divorced, heard about it as well. Their fears about his life choices were proving true.

We met at Jay's favorite fast-food place and sat down. He began unloading not only his present self-made predicament, but lots of other weights as well.

I first met Jay when he was 13. He was withdrawn, sullen, and not interested in God in any form. He came to church because his mom wanted him to be there.

I saw myself in that kid—capable, filled with turmoil, and angry. I began to try to build a relationship to gain his trust. I asked him to lunch and attended his games. He rejected all my efforts, but I simply never went away.

After several years we grew to know and trust each other, but he still had no desire for a relationship with Christ, something I longed for him to have. He continued to make poor choices—defiant, troubled choices.

He finally fell silent, and I delivered my best sermon ever: I said nothing. I just sat there, looking him in the eyes, giving him all the room he needed.

He couldn't take it after a bit and blurted, "What?"

"What?" I retorted.

"Well, aren't you going to chew me out?" he exclaimed, as if reaching the surface of the water out of breath and taking the first gulp of air.

Silence. I waited. "No. Why?" I asked. Another pause. "Haven't others already done that?"

He nodded.

"You know all you've done is wrong?"

Another nod.

I delivered my best sermon ever: I said nothing.

"Then why would I chew you out? I'm still here, and you are still loved."

Jay stared at his half-eaten sandwich.

"You don't have to look down in shame," I said. "I am still here." I leveraged all my years of investment into that one moment.

Jay's dam of resistance broke. He changed dramatically and quickly after that. Don't get me wrong—adolescent males always race with testosterone and boundless cravings for life and adventure. But Jay's heart and attitude changed principally toward God and toward me.

Seven years later I was on a train bound to see Jay and spend time with him again. No trouble this time; I would be officiating at his wedding. There were barbecues with his friends, late-night coffees, tons of laughter, and some cherished solo time for Jay and me to just hang out and not say a word. We reviewed the wedding plans and spoke about the future, about Jay's ambitions and emerging dreams.

I wrote Jay a letter and left it in his room to discover after I was gone. I had told him most of it before, but I've come to understand that even as adults, we men still need other men speaking in our lives. The main thing I wanted Jay to know through my letter was simple: I believe in him and always will.

—*Mike Brantley*

WHEN GOD BREAKS THROUGH

Sometimes God calls us out of our comfort zones to really love others, as Mike's story shows. Jesus challenged his listeners with these words: "If you love those who love you, what reward will you get? Are not even tax collectors doing that?" (Matthew 5:46, NIV). If you really want to love others, love those who aren't in a position to show love to you. Intentionally getting "in the way of relationships" is the essence of worship (Isaiah 58; Micah 6:8) and transforms lives. James, the brother of Jesus, knew all about how a relationship with the right person can transform a life. That's why he was able to write confidently, "My brothers, if any of you should wander away from the truth and another should turn him back on to the right path, then the latter may be sure that in turning a man back from his wandering course he has rescued a soul from death, and in so doing will 'cover a multitude of sins'" (James 5:20, PHI).

MY CHALLENGE

You can be a "spiritual parent" to someone, regardless of your age or whether you have children of your own or lack seminary training. All you need is a willingness to invest time in someone's life. Ask the Lord to open your eyes and heart to someone in whom you can invest. He may show you someone in your community, church, or workplace who needs the love. Pray also about any feelings of inadequacy you might feel. Remember that God can equip you for any task.

54 SLEEPLESS
Resting in the Lord

My heartbeat quickened, my throat grew dry, and I started to panic. I had suddenly realized that I was the lone adult in the house, and I had two tiny lives depending on me.

And that realization was the beginning of something alien to my life: sleeplessness.

I know sleep deprivation is no laughing matter, so I'd never let it happen to me. I'd always guarded my sleep by maintaining control of my life and the lives of those around me. Knowing I had everything managed and everyone organized helped me experience peace.

But then our second child was born right on the heels of the first. When my husband left on his next business trip, I realized I was alone in the house at night with two helpless infants. Each night I gently tucked them in their cribs, sang their favorite songs, left them with a comforting smile, and closed the door. They fell asleep easily, but I found it impossible to rest, haunted by my heavy responsibility.

As I paced the hallway, checking on each baby every few minutes, I became unable to settle down, much less sleep. What if one had trouble breathing? What if one tried to climb out of the crib? What if one needed something and couldn't cry for help? What if . . . what if . . . what if? How could I think about sleeping—not being alert, not watching, not being there if one of my children should need me?

I prayed for safety through the night, scolded myself for being so worried, and did everything I could to ensure my children's safety, but nothing calmed me. My inability to guarantee my children's safety through the night shook me to my foundation.

One night when I was up very late reading Scripture, I stumbled upon Psalm 121:

> I look up to the mountains—
> does my help come from there?
> My help comes from the LORD,
> who made heaven and earth!
> He will not let you stumble;
> the one who watches over you will not slumber.
> Indeed, he who watches over Israel
> never slumbers or sleeps.
> The LORD himself watches over you!
> The LORD stands beside you as your protective shade.
> The sun will not harm you by day,
> nor the moon at night.
> The LORD keeps you from all harm
>   and watches over your life.
> The LORD keeps watch over you as you come and go,
> both now and forever.
>
> —Psalm 121, NLT

I was both convicted and calmed by God's words. While I was frantically trying to ensure that I didn't let my children stumble, didn't let harm come to them, and didn't let them out of my sight, I was also playing god in my world. My trying to control everyone and everything was exhausting, and it wasn't working. I realized I am not God and cannot control every moment of my children's lives. Nor can I love my children as much as their Creator does. God's Word says the One who made the world never sleeps but watches and guards and protects us. I realized that because he never sleeps, I can sleep peacefully.

I immediately felt sleepy that night and woke up refreshed the next morning. Instead of obsessing about my children's bedtime, I started placing my children in their Creator's loving hands each night.

How could I think about sleeping—not being alert, not watching, not being there if one of my children should need me?

My children are much older now, and I hate to admit that I still worry about them. Homework, friends, drugs, alcohol, dates—yikes! They encounter so many opportunities to fail or to experience pain. But whenever I try to orchestrate my children's lives, that restless, panicky feeling from years ago returns. It's a small reminder that I need to loosen my grip and trust God with the people I love.

God's word has taught me who is in control. Each time I feel the urge to panic, I recite the words of Psalm 121 instead. Now I know I can sleep, because I know that my God never does.

—*Gloria Spielman*

WHEN GOD BREAKS THROUGH

We parents need to remind ourselves that we can't control everything that will happen to our children. We're meant to be our children's parents. But God's words reassure us that we can't be "super-parents." We can't protect our children from everything. God knows this desire and respects it. He also reminds us that instead of our being everything to our children, *he* is to be everything to our children. Every breath our children take is directed by their Creator; each heartbeat is monitored by the one who gave them life. He loves our children more than we ever could; therefore we can trust him with their well-being. We do what we can and we trust God for the rest, knowing that he "keeps watch over" us and them "both now and forever."

MY CHALLENGE

Pray through Psalm 121 for yourself, your children, or someone else whose burdens you shoulder. What words in that psalm bring you the most comfort? Write them down and keep them in a place where they will remind you of God's constant care for you and your loved ones.

55

BLUNDER DOWN UNDER

Understanding the Value of Friendships

Who would steal a pair of ordinary jeans? Well, maybe they weren't so ordinary because they were distinctly American style in a non-American country. Maybe someone else valued American products as much as I did. And I was truly clinging to everything American—because culture shock had set in.

After graduating from high school in Illinois, I was studying for a year at the University of Sydney in New South Wales, Australia. In the first few weeks, I had phoned home far too often, choked up and speechless for at least a minute each time I heard an American accent. In this strange land down under, people talked funny and drove on the wrong side of the street. Currency exchanges required higher mathematical reasoning than I possessed. Everything seemed so odd.

Somebody out there is wearing my clothes! Surely this is an omen to head back home . . .

I realized my pessimistic attitude kept me from making new friends. But I did help my boardinghouse roommates with their laundry. On days when my classes began in the late morning, I did my laundry and hung it out to dry. In the late afternoon after classes, I brought in my clothes and anyone else's hanging on the line, something all the girls in the house did for one another.

With 12 fashion-conscious girls, we always had lots of laundry. Twelve erratic schedules contributed to the piles of clothing waiting to be washed. Why do the laundry until you have nothing else to wear?

One day I came home, dropped my books, and went to bring in my dry clothes. As I stepped outside, I saw that the clotheslines were empty.

"Tracé, thanks for bringing in my wash!" I shouted to my roommate as I came back in the house.

"I didn't bring it in," she replied.

"Well, Vicki, thank *you* for bringing in my laundry," I said to another girl.

"I didn't bring in your clothes," Vicki said.

I checked with every girl in the house. No one had brought in my darks and whites. Doom and gloom set in. Could all my clothes have been stolen?

Those were my American jeans, my pretty blouses, my sentimental clothes. I felt violated and resentful.

Somebody out there is wearing my clothes! Combined with so many other cultural crises, it was the last straw. *Surely this is an omen to head back home,* I thought.

The housemistress arrived later that evening, and I decided to ask for her help. If anyone could get to the bottom of this, surely she could.

I approached her office timidly; she had a reputation for being stern and uncaring.

"My clothes were stolen." *There—I got it out without crying.*

"Oh, they were? Well, they're just rags," she sneered.

My jaw dropped. Did she just call my clothes *rags?*

"And rags can be replaced."

How insensitive!

I returned to my room, not knowing if I wanted to scream or cry. As I sat there and stewed, I realized after awhile just how right the housemistress was, even though she had been rather cold about it. Clothes could be replaced. I thought about the other valuable things in my life, and my mind focused on relationships. What mattered more: possessions or relationships?

The relationships at home that I had temporarily lost I would regain when my year in Australia ended. And I could gain meaningful new friendships here if I gave this place a chance.

Blundering fool, I scolded myself. *Wake up!*

I never saw my stolen "rags" again, but I did establish friendships in Australia that have flourished for decades—outlasting any pair of jeans! Seventeen Aussie friends bid farewell to me at the Sydney airport when this speechless, choked-up Yank headed home to Illinois. Several of them have visited me since then, two during their honeymoons! Even though we're continents apart, we continue to be part of each other's lives.

Like the ad says, a pair of jeans—$40. Newfound friends—priceless.

—Gabriella Filippi

When God Breaks Through

Sometimes it's tough to learn the larger-than-life lesson that we need to cherish people and relationships, not the stuff of this world. Those relationships are gifts from above. They are never to be taken for granted. But so often we jealously guard our possessions and treat relationships lightly. Consider the story of a man who came to Jesus wanting him to settle a family dispute. But instead Jesus warned: "Beware! Guard against every kind of greed. Life is not measured by how much you own" (Luke 12:15, NLT). Greed caused a wedge between the family members. But God reminds us over and over about the priceless value of people.

My Challenge

Have you ever thanked God for the people in your life? As you do that, consider the relationships where you might have allowed possessions or attitudes to take precedence: when you preferred watching your favorite show instead of talking to your spouse or the kids; when you mourned the loss of a favorite item and worried about it rather than the fact that you yelled at a family member for breaking or losing it. Do you need to reconcile with someone this week? Ask God for the courage to do so.

56

FIREFLIES

Grasping the Truth of God's Persistence and Presence

This has been a difficult day, I realized with a bit of surprise. I didn't know why it had seemed tough—nothing specifically bad had happened. Maybe it was because I felt like I couldn't get off the merry-go-round I seemed to be riding. As a newlywed I loved my new life, but I also felt a little . . . off. So much had changed in two months that I wasn't sure how to handle it all—a new husband, a new job, bills to pay, no longer living near my closest friends, and living in a tiny apartment that I couldn't manage to keep clean. In the middle of all the busyness, I felt lonely.

A tiny breeze teased me out into the humid July evening. I decided a quick walk would clear my head, and so I wandered to my favorite corner in town, 15 minutes away from our apartment. I go to that corner to chase sunsets—it's the best view within miles, and I love watching the colors reflect off the clouds above the trees.

Only a few other walkers were around, and the night was quiet. After watching the sun slip into darkness, I turned to head home. Caught up in thoughts of bills and wondering how anyone ever has enough money to purchase a house, I pondered how many of our apartments could fit inside the house on the corner. *Probably seven,* I mused.

Out of nowhere I saw a firefly and gasped. The first sighting of fireflies always signified summer for me. Even though we were well into summer this was the first firefly I'd seen, and I knew I had to adhere to the rule that my little sister and I lived by as kids: Whenever you see the first firefly of summer, you have to try to catch it.

Back then Claire and I would run to the backyard with a peanut butter jar, ready to chase fireflies. Mom and Dad dutifully prepared the jar for us in advance, complete with holes in the lid. They left it on the counter beginning in May so we could grab it at a moment's notice with the thrill of the first sighting.

And so when we would see the first flickering light in the backyard, it was ritual: Barefoot in the soft grass, we fumbled in our dark yard to find and gently catch the glowing creatures always miraculous to our young eyes. We lived on almost an acre, and I remember chases for one firefly or another that would take us all the way around the house, as we laughed and shrieked the entire way. We would arrive out of breath at the place where we began, amazed at the tiny bugs' elusiveness.

Three more times I tried the same thing: walk, shake, try to lose the firefly.

Even though I am older and have longer limbs, fireflies still elude my grasp. That night during my walk the chase was different. As I reached for the firefly, it didn't resist. Instead it slowed its fluttering wings and landed on my hand. I stopped, amazed. After admiring my skill in catching the firefly, I was ready to move on with my walk. Apparently the firefly wasn't.

As I continued my strides, it stayed with me, unfazed by my movement. After 10 feet I tried to shake it off, thinking it odd that it remained with me. It then flew to my forearm. Three more times I tried the same thing: walk, shake, try to lose the firefly. And three more times the firefly repeated its dance: flutter, hover, and relocate—always to a different part of my arm.

I finally moved the stubborn creature to my index finger and brought it near my eyes. What tiny legs, what delicate feelers. As I pondered the miracle that it was, God spoke to my heart.

I am with you. Just like this firefly refuses to leave you, so do I. I will always stay with you, even when you want to shake me off, even when you aren't sure why I stay.

I was stunned. I hadn't thought about God that evening. I had thought about the sunset, the bills we needed to pay, the firefly—but not God. Something in my heart warmed, and I understood that God knew I was lonely. When I was worried about everything *but* him, he had been thinking about me.

I started walking again and the firefly finally flew away, but I knew that God was still with me. Although everything else in my life was changing, I was reminded that night that no matter what, God stays the same. Like a firefly on the first night of summer, he is constantly beautiful, majestic, and present. He shines the brightest when we reach the darkest parts of our lives—and although we may try to catch him, he is actually the one catching us with his love.

—*Ann Swindell*

WHEN GOD BREAKS THROUGH

Ever do the great "shake off" with God as Ann did? When it comes to getting a person's attention, God wrote the book on persistence. While reminding us of his presence, he persists until we finally absorb the fact that he will never leave us.

During Old Testament times, God reminded Moses and the Israelites of the gift of his presence: "My Presence will go with you, and I will give you rest" (Exodus 33:14, NIV). Like many gifts, this gift wasn't always appreciated—that is, until the next hardship appeared. During those times realization that God was with them was a comforting port in a storm.

MY CHALLENGE

When are you most tempted to doubt that God is with you? Can you think of a time when God showed you that he was there? If God is making you aware of his presence right now, thank him for being with you. What do you think he's teaching you through the knowledge that he is near you?

57 A DIVINE EMBRACE
Finding God's Comfort in a Child's Hug

I jolted awake as the phone by my bed rang.

I answered the call on the third ring without time to contemplate what the news might be—a church member in jail? A teenager running away from home? A medical emergency at the hospital?

But it was my oldest sister, Ann. "Rick, Mother has been admitted to the hospital. Her heart stopped, but the doctors revived her. She is holding on by a thread."

Unlike Daddy, who died 15 years earlier of a sudden, massive heart attack, my mother had frequently stared death in the face. For three years, Mother had been in the hospital every other month with congestive heart failure. But Ann's quivering voice told me this was frightening and urgent.

"Hurry, Rick. The doctors are giving her very little hope."

I booked a flight from Chicago to Huntsville, Alabama, for the next morning. The two-hour flight seemed like an eternity, and I arrived expecting the worst. I knew Mother had instructed the doctors and nurses not to resuscitate her if her heart failed.

As a pastor I was used to hospitals. But this time I walked into the cardiac care unit as a son, and the 83-year-old woman lying in bed No. 6 with tubes running in and out of her body was my mother.

My mother. With a switch from a bush outside the back door she disciplined us when my twin brother and I were disobedient, but she always hugged us afterward and affirmed something good. When Daddy lost his job, she reminded all of us that things would work out, and they did. And when Daddy started a shoe store as a second career, she worked tirelessly with him all day and came home to household chores at night. She supported my call to ministry. Even though I was shy, she saw abilities that others had not seen.

Mother was breathing but barely conscious when I walked into the CCU. She had always been strong, and now she demonstrated a similar valor in the face of death. Each day as our family gathered we asked, "Will this be the day?"

Yet Mother hung on. She was a fighter.

A week after my arrival in Huntsville, my wife and seven-year-old daughter, Bailey, arrived. My niece was getting married in Huntsville that weekend and Bailey was the flower girl. The wedding, planned months in advance, was joyous despite our family's sorrow that Mother was fighting for her life.

Before the wedding I stole some time away from the festivities to be with Mother.

"I love you," she said.

I stroked her hand. "I love you too."

The next morning Mother's heart finally gave out. Per her directive, the nurses did not resuscitate her. She was home.

"She's gone," my oldest brother, Jerry, said as I arrived at the hospital.

I felt dazed. I walked to a waiting area that looked east over the city and toward the foothills of the Appalachian Mountains. I saw Monte Sano jutting into a sky of magnificent blue, the sun glistening. But the beauty could not console my broken heart.

Mother, I can't believe you're gone! You were strength, encouragement, stability, wisdom—all that the word "mother" implies.

I tried to remain strong. After all, pastors are supposed to be stalwart in a crisis. But at that moment this pastor was a son who had just lost his mother. And my tears flowed.

"Daddy!" I turned, and my daughter leaped into my arms. Bailey clutched my neck, her legs wrapped around my waist. She didn't say a word. I'm not sure if I was holding her or she was holding me. But it was exactly what I needed.

I needed human contact. Bailey was hurting because her dad was hurting.

I needed human contact. Bailey was hurting because her dad was hurting. In her embrace I felt love and care. As my mother had often embraced her son, now my daughter was embracing her father. And in that moment something transcendent happened. While my daughter was comforting me through her embrace, I felt the embrace of another.

Amazingly, I felt the touch of Jesus.

—*Rick Ezell*

When God Breaks Through

Pain has a way of eclipsing the reality of Jesus' presence, much as the moon hides the sun in a solar eclipse. Yet sometimes he makes his presence known if we are not looking for something miraculous or spectacular and are able to receive him in the midst of the mundane and the seemingly insignificant. Even when we can't see God, we can sense his comforting arms buoying us through the seas of sorrow.

My Challenge

Often we mistakenly think God's comfort means that our troubles will go away. Nothing can take away the loss of a loved one, the pain of a divorce, or the sting of rejection. But we can extend God's comfort to others through simple acts—a hug, our presence, a listening ear. As Paul wrote in 2 Corinthians 1:3–4: "All praise to the God and Father of our Lord Jesus Christ. He is the source of every mercy and the God who comforts us. He comforts us in all our troubles so that we can comfort others. When others are troubled, we will be able to give them the same comfort God has given us" (NLT).

Think of how you have been comforted during times of difficulty. Write a note, send an e-mail, or call that person to say thanks for being there.

58 MISS(ED) HOSPITALITY

Learning to Open Heart and Home

I motioned my guest into a house smelling of cleaner and burned banana muffins. On my hip I balanced my baby daughter, wearing only a leg cast and a diaper. I had planned for a much nicer scene when my college roommate had phoned early that morning.

"I'm driving through your area today," Gayle revealed. "Could I stop to visit?"

Ever since I left the corporate world and traded my designer shoes and PDA for fuzzy slippers and a diaper bag, I had searched to find where I fit in the world. When my roommate called, I thought it was God's Big Plan for my life, appearing like sunlight slicing through my fog. Hospitality! Angels sang! Perhaps I was in such a place as my home at such a time as this so that God could develop in me a buried—very deeply buried—gift

for hospitality! Surely my college friend would be the first of legions to find renewal as I brewed tea, brought out china cups, and offered coffee cake.

"Please come," I urged. "I'll bake goodies."

"See you midmorning," Gayle confirmed.

"No problem at all," I replied.

But I did have a problem. As I hung up the phone, I glanced at my toddler who had broken her leg the day before. The orthopedic surgeon had told me to keep her leg immobile and elevated for the next six weeks. But I figured I could bake, clean, and keep a toddler's leg elevated with no problem—after all I had just been crowned Miss Hospitality! So I started off with a simple list—bake, clean, and keep my daughter comfortable.

I slipped my daughter into a frilly dress and fastened her into the high chair. By extending the footrest, I both immobilized and elevated her leg. Brilliant! She could flip through picture books while I baked banana muffins. I seized a recipe, mixed and poured batter, and slid a muffin tin into the oven.

Smugly washing bowls and spatulas, I congratulated myself at how easily I had juggled my culinary, medical, and maternal responsibilities while keeping my darling happy and occupied. Very occupied, I realized, because I had not heard her squeal for several minutes.

Then I smelled a new aroma mingling with that of the baking muffins.

I turned around.

My daughter had overfilled her diaper. Never one to miss a finger-painting opportunity, she had dipped her hands into the new art medium and traced swirling patterns on the high chair tray. She smeared the overflow onto her face and dress and painted her arms, hair, and books. She also added decorative touches to the nearby kitchen wall.

Horrified, I began chanting a checklist as I sprinted out of the kitchen carrying my angel at arms' length.

Clean her and diaper her. Keep the cast dry.

That accomplished, I tucked Baby under my arm and like a running back carrying a pigskin, I tore through the house.

Toss soiled dress into bathroom sink and turn on cold water for soaking. Dump diaper and "painted" books into garage garbage. Scrub "artwork" from wall.

In a desperate moment, I invented "the one-armed-heave," a new competitive event for transporting fiberglass high chairs into backyards.

Hold onto Baby and untangle the garden hose. Spray the high chair and tray. Sprinkle them with cleanser.

The fragrance of burning muffins greeted me when I returned to the kitchen.

Pull charred treats from the oven.

Then I remembered the dress. I arrived in the bathroom to find dirty water cascading from a sink that, until that day, had not trapped water since the Reagan administration.

Turn off the tap. Sit Baby in her room. Fetch the least burned muffin for her to chew. Sponge mop the bathroom carpet and open the window. Check on Baby.

Sit Baby in her room. Fetch the least burned muffin for her to chew.

My daughter was far more mobile in her cast than I anticipated. She also displayed excellent fine-motor skills. Instead of eating the muffin, she reduced it to crumbs and, like a flower girl strewing petals, distributed them throughout her bedroom.

Vacuum nursery carpet.

I eyed the drying bathroom carpet and vacuumed it too, only to hear a sound like that of a 747 lowering its landing gear. The vacuum cleaner groaned to a halt. I abandoned it in the hallway.

Check the clock. Scrub hands. Pop more muffins into the oven.

Next I scooped up my daughter, grabbed the wet dress, and hurried to the downstairs family room.

Slip Sesame Street *videotape into the VCR. Plop Baby onto the couch. Wedge pillow under her cast. Throw dress into the washing machine.*

On my way to the laundry room, I spied the brown water dripping through the ceiling from the bathroom above.

I slumped to the ground, defeated, clutching the dripping dress. I had scrubbed, mopped, washed, and vacuumed more than if my mother-in-law were visiting and was less prepared for my guest than when I had started. "If you are calling me to this, God, then why can't I do it right?" I demanded.

The doorbell rang.

Gayle jokes that she spent the following ten years teaching English in China to avoid another dose of my hospitality. I laugh with her because I know that God really does intend for me to be hospitable, but his take is a bit different. He asks that I open my door and share what I have. I've found that friendships—and memories—grow even sweeter when what you share is a little burned around the edges.

—*Martha Manikas-Foster*

WHEN GOD BREAKS THROUGH

> Above all, love each other deeply, because love covers over a multitude of sins. Offer hospitality to one another without grumbling. Each one should use whatever gift he has received to serve others, faithfully administering God's grace in its various forms (1 Peter 4:8–10, NIV).

What does *hospitality* mean to you? Does it mean a spotless home, a well-scrubbed (and well-behaved) child, and special food? That's not the type of hospitality Peter referred to in these verses. Christian hospitality doesn't focus on the host. Rather, it focuses on the needs of the guest—whether the guest needs a hot meal, a warm bed, or just a place to sit and be encouraged. When we focus on that type of hospitality, it doesn't matter whether our house is messy or if the offered snack is a can of soup.

MY CHALLENGE

Think about the last time you had guests over. List your main concerns in preparing for the visit and during the visit. Look over your list and mark each concern with a *Y* for You, if the concern is more about how you (and your house) appear, and a *G* for Guest, if it was a concern about your guests' needs. Based on what you discover, think of ways you can offer the type of hospitality Peter talked about.

59

THE LITTLE MOTHER

Learning to Cope Through Life's Difficulties

"I'm next!" my younger sister shouted.

"No, you're not!" my older sister yelled.

"Girls, stop arguing. You'll each get your turn," Mom said.

We were making doughnuts. Mom could fit only two punched-out dough forms on the top of the bubbling oil at one time. We crowded around the kitchen table, where we watched the dough sink to the bottom, sizzle, and then pop up to the surface.

Mom did lots of stuff with us when we were young even though she had her hands full with three girls. Chris was three years older than me, and Judy was two years younger. Mom fixed wonderful meals and often sang to her pet yellow canary in the cage in the corner of the kitchen. They both whistled and warbled, with Mom matching Tweety's high-pitched tone.

But the year I turned 10, something changed.

Our baby brother, Peter, was born that year. He was cute, with a shock of blond hair, dark chocolate eyes, and a sweet smile.

Shortly after he was born, Mom's body became crippled with rheumatoid arthritis. First her toes began curling up. Then her fingers became gnarled claws. After a while she couldn't even stretch them out straight. She saw doctor after doctor but came home from those visits crying with pain and frustration because the doctors couldn't do much. She could no longer walk easily. And the worst challenge for her was taking care of my baby brother.

I didn't understand what was going on. I wanted my old mom back. I missed her braiding my hair, the great dinners she used to make, and the homemade doughnuts. And she didn't sing anymore.

One night I was in bed with my pink and white bedspread pulled up to my chin. I hadn't fallen asleep yet when I heard Peter crying. He was in his crib in the nursery, sniffling and squawking as babies do when they're hungry or wet. I waited for Mom to get up and take care of him. And I waited some more. Either she didn't hear him or she couldn't get out of bed.

Go to him, a voice whispered in my head.

I didn't want to listen. And I didn't want to get out of my warm bed. Didn't my older sister hear him? Her room was right next to his. But nobody got up to help.

Then I heard it again. *Go to him.*

So I tossed off the covers and walked down the long hallway to the other end of the house. He was still crying. Restless. Wet maybe? I checked his

Go to him, a voice whispered in my head.

diaper. Dry. I rubbed his back and whispered soothing words I'd heard Mom do when he was fussy. Eventually he fell asleep. I padded back to my room and quietly slipped into bed.

The next morning no one said a word about that night. I was a little tired, but I made the best of it. I had no idea that I probably wouldn't get a full night's sleep for quite a while.

Peter cried almost every night. When he did, I got up and soothed him. I knew Mom was in pain, but why couldn't she take care of her own son? Why did I have to do it? But I just couldn't ignore that soft voice telling me to *go to him*, even though I wanted to. Eventually I started caring for him not just at night but also during the day.

I became what the family called "the little mother." I took my brother for walks, played with him in the park, and picked up every toy he tossed out his playpen. When he was older we sat together on the floor and built Lego airplanes and Lincoln Log houses.

Some things I learned by trial and error. Like the afternoon I walked out of the family room and left the screen door open to the backyard. I just went into the kitchen for a minute to make a peanut butter and jelly sandwich. When I came back my little brother was gone. He'd toddled out the door, around the side of the house, and down the driveway. I got to him just before he wobbled into the street.

Mom tried treatment after treatment to stop the pain. Eventually she had surgery—lots of surgery to replace the joints in all her fingers and toes. She could no longer handle diaper pins and tiny shoelaces.

I accepted the fact that taking care of my brother was my job, but it wasn't always easy. Sometimes I couldn't stop for pizza after school with my friends because of my responsibilities. Sometimes family members helped and that was good. But during the nights—the long and sometimes difficult nights—I heard the voice that whispered *go to him* yet again.

Mom's hands and feet got better after all her operations and she learned to live within her limitations. She even started singing again. When I think about all the pain she went through, I am amazed that she could be as joyful and as good a mother as she was.

Peter grew up and turned out OK, and so did I. All those years of caring for him were great practice for when I married and had my own sons.

Sometimes I wonder how I did it, being a little mother from the age of 10. But I was never alone. And I'm still not alone. When I listen to that gentle voice, I hear Jesus leading the way.

—*B. J. Taylor*

WHEN GOD BREAKS THROUGH

Ever feel overwhelmed at the enormity of a task before you? Although B. J. felt out of her depth and alone, she later discovered that she was neither. Like the Old Testament prophet to whom God called (see 1 Samuel 3), B. J. obeyed, later learning that God called and equipped her to do the job at hand.

Writing to a group of beleaguered believers in the Roman colony of Philippi, the Apostle Paul provided watchwords for the overwhelmed or overworked: "I can do everything through Christ, who gives me strength" (Philippians 4:13, NLT).

MY CHALLENGE

When have you felt completely out of your depth? If you feel overwhelmed by the amount of work you have to complete, consider the message of Philippians 4:13. Write a list of your tasks. As you think about these, ask God for the strength to do everything "through Christ."

60 A FRIEND FEW CAN CLAIM

Reaping the Power of Daily Prayer

"You know, Mark, I have prayed for you every day since you were 15."

I remember the day my friend Frank told me this, a few years ago after a game of racquetball.

Frank was 24 years old when we met, a married Bible college student and the new youth director at my midtown Detroit church. I was a 15-year-old high school freshman, new to the youth group, who thought of girls with wondrous attraction and desperate fear.

Frank and his wife had their first child that year. "Diapers! Crying! Cute, but later!" my friends and I thought. The nine years between Frank and me seemed like a pretty wide gap. But Frank had a gift for bridging gulfs.

Once he treated a wondrous female and me to pizza after a youth group meeting. Just the three of us talking, laughing, and chowing (my specialty). Besides being in tune with our social lives, Frank could throw a baseball harder and hit farther than any of us. In pickup football he dodged and darted with such remarkable quickness that even by triple-teaming him we couldn't prevent his interceptions and catches.

And of course Frank was committed to our spiritual well-being. He led our group through a study of 1 Corinthians, which was probably one of the courses he was studying at Bible college. Firmly grounded in his own commitment to love and serve Jesus Christ, Frank built a bond with us. He prayed with us, planned and worked, and showed us that the gospel captured all of him. He displayed the fact that the best life was to know Christ in word, deed, worship, pizza, and family.

And then, after only one year, he was gone—studies done and a different job awaiting. Frank and his wife moved, and we didn't see them much anymore. But he left an indelible impression.

Years passed. I found good work. I found love, raised children, and did my gig as camp counselor and youth soccer coach and mentor to the young. Occasionally I heard about Frank, still doing statewide bike tours with youth groups, still passionately building relationships in churches. I was always grateful for that year he spent at Central Northwest Church, for his model of Christian faith.

Frank has moved again . . . But I'm sure his daily prayers for me continue.

Forty years passed before we met again. I joined the faculty of a Christian college about an hour's drive from a small church Frank pastored. We connected through a phone call and agreed to meet.

Frank hadn't changed much. He was still eager to serve God, know God, love people, smile, work, and pray through whatever darkness or light the day presented. We decided to regularly meet at the college's racquetball court.

And so we met to play racquetball, share breakfast, and pray. Frank was still athletic, but slower than the last time we faced off. Now his nine years of seniority worked in my favor. His racquetball stroke was sure and strong. He'd whip me on service. My feet were faster than his. I'd whip him on side shots, enough to trade wins and wipeouts.

I'm sure the robust youth on the other courts wondered at us two gray hairs who enjoyed hitting a well-placed ball and laughed and talked and prayed, as old friends do when they're bonded in Christ.

Frank has moved again, and our racquetball mornings have ended. But I'm sure his daily prayers for me continue. Frank prayed for me for years without my asking. Few people are blessed with a friend like that.

—Mark Fackler

When God Breaks Through

Consistency is one of the sustaining forces of a relationship. God wants his people to exhibit the same level of consistency in their relationships with him. Speaking through the prophet Isaiah, God invites us to come before him: "Give ear and come to me; hear me, that your soul may live" (Isaiah 55:3, NIV). Not only will we live, but also those we bring to God in prayer may experience the same life. Praying consistently can be difficult—we tend to let other things take precedence. But the rewards of consistent time with God can be life changing and life defining.

My Challenge

Are you spending time with God each day? If not, are you willing to make that commitment? Consider also committing to pray for someone consistently. Thank God for those who pray for you each day.

61 TURKEY AND TROUBLE
Tapping Into God's Amazing Peace

I dreaded the thought of Thanksgiving. My dad had left home and my parents were divorcing. I hated to admit it, but I was glad to be away at school so I could escape the tension. It was easier to deal with my parents' pain over the phone than face-to-face.

Soon Thanksgiving would arrive and I'd have to go home. Any day is difficult when a family is falling apart, and the worst normal days are mild compared to a holiday. The seat is empty where someone used to sit. And all those familiar rituals. All the sentimentality. All the hopes of love and togetherness. I dreaded the trip home more every day and couldn't find one thing about the holiday to look forward to.

I remembered a passage from Philippians and quoted it to myself over and over: "Be careful for nothing; but in everything by prayer and supplication, let your requests be made known unto God. And the peace of God, which passes all understanding, will keep your hearts and minds through Christ Jesus."

I wasn't experiencing the promised peace. At other times I'd experienced God's peace through difficult circumstances, but not this time. What was wrong? I felt as if I needed something more, some push, some *something* that would give me the faith to face the holidays and all the family conflict and disappointment I would have to walk through.

One dreary day I flipped through my Bible looking for something encouraging. I decided to read the verse that I'd been quoting and was greatly surprised to find that I'd left out a phrase. The passage actually read: "Be careful for nothing; but in everything by prayer and supplication *with thanksgiving* let your requests be made known unto God. And the peace of God, which passeth all understanding, shall keep your hearts and minds through Christ Jesus (Philippians 4:6–7 KJV, emphasis added).

With thanksgiving. With Thanksgiving? *With thanksgiving!*

What irony. I know that *thanksgiving* as it is used in that verse simply means "gratitude." What a fluke that the very phrase I left out included the name of the holiday that caused me so much anxiety. But it was a funny, apropos fluke.

Through this, God let me know that his presence and peace are very specific. Like a secret code or a wink that only you and someone else understand,

> *I dreaded the trip home more every day, and couldn't find one thing about the holiday to look forward to.*

this was an inside joke between God and me: Even during this dreaded Thanksgiving holiday, he was big enough to bring me peace beyond my understanding.

I read that Scripture and laughed. Out loud. Right there with my Bible on my lap. I laughed for the first time in a long time. It was so nice to escape the pain for a while. Not only could I put aside my worries and ask for God's help, but I could also still feel grateful for my life. And I could even do it during a family holiday when the toughest part of my life would be impossible to ignore.

With thanksgiving. That one little phrase was the kicker for my turnaround. I kept praying, journaling, and preparing for the holiday, and that moment between gave me a taste of the peace God offers. I knew that with him I was OK, even though nothing around me felt OK.

As I had expected, Thanksgiving that year was not fun, nor were the holidays that followed. But I've never forgotten that weird little moment when misquoting the Bible set me up for a good laugh with God and gave me peace in the toughest times.

—*Carol Smith*

WHEN GOD BREAKS THROUGH

Pain and grief seem huge when you're enveloped in these emotions. The upheaval stretches over your life like a dark cloud. But not only is God bigger than your pain, your life is bigger than that pain too. When pain or grief threatens to rain on your parade, God offers the umbrella of his peace and strength. "The LORD will give strength to His people; the LORD will bless His people with peace" (Psalm 29:11, NKJV). The writer of that psalm, King David, experienced family dysfunction, which caused him to rely heavily on God. In our weakness he is strong (see 2 Corinthians 12:9).

MY CHALLENGE

Boldly ask for peace, even if you have trouble believing that God will supply it. Then soak it in when it comes. Receiving God's peace doesn't mean you won't experience the pain and sorrow of a hard situation. But it does remind you that you're not alone.

62 ALL THINGS NEW
Finding New Beginnings in Brokenness

Carefully I opened the box from Japan so I could place my treasures in my new home.

I knew the beautiful glass bowl my husband and I had received on our wedding day would be on top.

Instead I only found shards of glass, my lovely prize now shattered.

Just like me, I thought, as I released the tears I'd fought all day. *God, how could you let this happen to me?*

So much had been shattered in such a short time that my head spun. My husband and I had been missionaries together for ten years in Japan. But then he'd left me. My marriage and ministry were suddenly both shattered, as were all my plans and dreams for the future.

God, how could you let this happen to me?

My two-year-old daughter reached up for me to hold her and hid her face on my shoulder. She was still clinging to me as I talked on the phone with the man in charge of the ministry that provided apartments for single mothers. I tried to answer his questions clearly, but everything seemed surreal. *How can I be a single mother? I so often counseled single mothers as part of my ministry in Japan, but now I'm one.*

As I looked out the window of my small apartment, I realized my life did not look anything like I had imagined it would. Even the landscape was a far cry from what I was used to. For some reason only known to him, God directed my children and me to Chicago for a fresh start, a new beginning.

Block after block of bare brown trees stood naked against a gray slate sky. Icy roads. Acres of frozen lawns smeared with dirty gray. I had grown up in sunny California, and winter in Chicago seemed even more foreign than my home in Japan. Just looking at the dismal landscape all around me, I felt very alone.

Well, not quite alone. Many kind people helped us move into our new home. Gifts and furniture and clothing mysteriously poured in, and I was overwhelmed by the generosity of God's people. I was thankful to be welcomed by so many new friends, but relieved when the final person left that first night.

God, how could you let this happen to me? . . .

How can I be a single mother?

I made a cup of tea. A new set of silverware was neatly stacked in a drawer, and new dishes—including new bowls—filled the shelves. *One by one the things I have lost are being replaced by something new,* I realized, finally paying heed to a gentle voice in my heart that I had refused to hear all day.

See, Colleen, the voice said, *I make all things new.*

"It's just hard to accept, Lord," I said. After all, I did not ask to be made new. I was quite happy with my life the way it had been.

Months went by. I slowly began to adapt to the new things God was doing. My son, who had been diagnosed with autism, was enrolled in a wonderful school where he quickly progressed, developing skills I had felt helpless to teach him before. This help was something I knew he would not have received in Japan.

Then God surprised me with the discovery that I could impact people through my writing and drawing. He sent mentors and led me to becoming a freelance writer and illustrator. Though my heart still missed my ministry to the people I loved in Japan, I found comfort and solace in painting and writing.

Three years have now passed since the bowl of my life was broken. When my husband left me, when I was uprooted from a ministry that I loved, even when I received welfare before moving to Chicago—these things did not happen because God was angry with me, as I once had wondered. I have accepted and learned to rest in the fact that although I've endured great pain, I've seen tremendous transformation. And this new form that I am in is a bowl that pleases him.

—Colleen Yang

When God Breaks Through

So many people face brokenness and renewal. It is easy to become set in our ways and confident in our goals. We believe we know what is best for our lives. So it's difficult when God shatters our expectations. We often have a difficult time accepting this, especially at the beginning of this process when change is usually so painful.

We can rest assured, however, that just because one story is over in our lives, we are not at the end of the book. In fact we may find a brand-new and even greater story to follow. With this knowledge we don't need to fight God, but we can rest in his hands knowing he is creating something new in us—something that's undoubtedly better than what we've known before.

My Challenge

Read the following verses from the Book of Jeremiah:

> The Lord gave another message to Jeremiah. He said, "Go down to the shop where clay pots and jars are made. I will speak to you while you are there." So I did as He told me and found the potter working at his wheel. Bu the jar he was making did not turn out as he had hoped, so the potter squashed the jar into a lump of clay and started again. Then the Lord gave me this message, "O Israel, can I not do to you as this potter has done to his clay? As the clay is in the potter's hand, so are you in my hand" (Jeremiah 18:1–6, NLT).

Reflect on those instances when God has molded you and redirected the course of your life, making it better than you could have planned. Write down some of these memories as reminders to yourself. If you are in the midst of a shattering time, pour out your heart to the Lord, and ask him to help you rest in his hands while he remakes your life.

AUTHORS

Mike Brantley leads a missional community, La Communauté, in New Orleans. He and his wife, Susanne, are on staff with Church Resource Ministries, in Communitas, which is focused on reaching the vast number of people beyond the reach of the existing church.

Tom Burggraf lives in Gunnison, Colorado, with his wife, Cherie, and their two children, Tommy and Quincy. He is Vice President of Institutional Advancement for Western State College of Colorado, interim pastor of Bethany Baptist Church, and a freelance writer and speaker.

Vicki Cairns has an M.A. in Intercultural Studies and TESOL (Teaching English to Speakers of Other Languages) from Wheaton College. She has a passion for people and interpersonal relationships and would like to explore ways to combine her interpersonal and intercultural expertise to offer hope and healing to individuals, especially women. She lives in Wheaton, Illinois.

Barbara O. Collier is a volunteer chaplain in women's jail ministry in Anderson, Indiana, where she lives. She is a grandmother of five beautiful grandchildren, enjoys swimming, and has a passion for God's Word.

Judith Costello lives with her family and numerous animals at a rural New Mexico farm. She is a full-time writer, artist, blogger, and mom.

Jeanette Dall is a freelance writer and former elementary school teacher who has written stories, puzzles, devotionals, and games for children and adults. Jeanette and her husband, Roger, live in Carol Stream, Illinois.

Christine Collier Erickson is a freelance writer living in Wheaton, Illinois. She enjoys hiking and biking with her husband and two children.

Rick Ezell is a husband, father, author, pastor, consultant, coach, conference leader, and communicator. Rick has a Doctor of Ministry in Preaching from Northern Baptist Theological Seminary. He has published more than 450 articles and sermons in various Christian publications. While authoring six books he has served more than twenty years in pastoral ministry. Rick, his wife, Cindy, and their daughter, Bailey, reside in Greer, South Carolina.

Mark Fackler is professor of communication at Calvin College, Grand Rapids, Michigan. He is author of several books and chapters, articles, and scripts. He calls balls and strikes at high school baseball games and teaches regularly at Daystar University in Nairobi. He is married with three sons.

Carol R. Fielding is a freelance writer and home-schooling mom. She lives in rural northwestern Pennsylvania with her husband, Bruce, and their three daughters. When she isn't writing or teaching, she can be found contentedly weeding one of her gardens.

Gabriella D. Filippi is a writer and speaker, business owner, and health consultant. She has written for major publications and newspapers. Gabriella lives in the western suburbs of Illinois.

Crista V. Forstrom chairs the Discipleship Ministry and leads the prayer team at the Covenant Church of Easton in Easton, Connecticut. Crista works part-time as a physical therapist and is also pursuing a Master of Divinity degree at Alliance Theological Seminary in Nyack, New York. She resides in Trumbull, Connecticut, with her husband, Chuck, and two small children, Kylie and Tyler.

Martha Manikas-Foster is a writer who works as a feature reporter for the *Family Life Network,* a radio network that broadcasts in New York and Pennsylvania. Her articles and devotionals have appeared in several national magazines. She lives in western New York state with her husband, David, and their children, Connie and Peter.

Jill N. Greer is a freelance writer and is actively involved in the prayer ministry at her church. She is the mother of three teenagers and resides in Trumbull, Connecticut.

Kent Keller is the pastor of Kendall Presbyterian Church in Miami, Florida. He is a writer, a sought-after speaker, as well as the father of four.

Linda MacKillop is the mother of four sons and nearing the empty-nest stage of life. She works as a freelance writer and enjoys writing fiction, nonfiction, and drama. Linda and her husband recently relocated from Virginia to the Chicago area where they love exploring the city and getting outdoors when the temperature rises above freezing.

Clarissa Moll's writing has appeared in various printed and online publications. She has taught communications-related courses at Cedarville University and Wheaton College. Ms. Moll lives with her family in Glendale Heights, Illinois.

Jennifer Morgan is a veteran communicator, author, and teacher. She currently serves as the Director of 3Story™ for Youth for Christ/USA where she has ministered for 23 years, training hundreds of ministers, youth pastors, and volunteers around the world. She loves learning how to follow Jesus more faithfully.

Heather Pleier lives with her husband in Germany. Taking a break from teaching English, she enjoys writing and exploring the European countryside.

Maggie Wallem Rowe is a writer, speaker, and dramatist who lives in the western suburbs of Chicago. She has been married to Mike, a pastor, for more than 30 years. Her greatest joy is that their children are walking in the truth.

Alison Simpson is a freelance writer and full-time mother of two elementary school-aged kids. She lives in Frankfort, Kentucky, where her husband, Tim, is a minister at a local Baptist church.

Gene R. Smillie is a cross-cultural educator and missionary. He has worked in Europe, Africa, and South America, and among a wide variety of cultures in North America, as a university professor and pastor.

Carol Smith is a freelance writer and songwriter living in Nashville, TN in a fixer upper home with two contented cats and two happy and (unexpectedly) large dogs.

Heidi Spencer is a freelance writer currently residing in Dayton, Ohio. Her husband, William, is a U.S. Air Force chaplain, and they are the proud parents of two children. Heidi has written dozens of news and feature articles for various newspapers, magazines, and nonprofit organizations. Heidi also serves her local church, Fairhaven Church, in Centerville, Ohio, as the Director of Special Needs Ministries.

Gloria R. Spielman is happily married for 24 years and the mother of two boys, one in college and one in middle school. She is a freelance writer, teaches women's Bible studies at her church, and sings on the church worship team. Her hobbies are working in her yard, maintaining a salt-water coral reef tank, playing hammered dulcimer and electric bass, reading classic mysteries, and studying Christian literature.

Ann Swindell is a writer who lives and works in the Chicago suburbs with her husband, Michael. A graduate of Wheaton College, she is currently working on her Master in Writing degree at DePaul University.

B. J. Taylor is an award-winning author whose work has appeared in *Guideposts,* many *Chicken Soup* books, and numerous magazines and newspapers. She has a wonderful husband, four children, and two adorable grandsons.

Sherrie Wilson and her husband, Neil, live in rural Wisconsin where she teaches fifth grade while he writes. Some of their best memories come from 13 years' service in a country church in Eureka, Wisconsin. Neil has authored and contributed to numerous books and specialty Bibles produced by the Livingstone Corporation.

Sharon Wright holds a degree in Business Administration from Cedarville University. She works in finance with The Evangelical Alliance Mission (TEAM) and is involved in various ministries with her church. She has two married daughters and lives in West Chicago, Illinois.

Colleen Yang, a former missionary to Japan, is a freelance writer and illustrator living in Carol Stream, Illinois, with her two children, Isaac and Lydia. She is fluent in Japanese and enjoys writing music.

Karen Young is a freelance writer who especially enjoys writing poetry. She was inspired as a child by the rich preaching, poetic, and music traditions of African American culture. In her leisure time, Karen also enjoys spending time with friends, singing, reading, and traveling.

Betsy Zenz is a freelance writer and editor. She lives in Boulder, Colorado with her husband, Andy, and daughter, Mercy.

Topical Index

Adoption
A Special Girl 206
Transformed by Love. 184

Affirmation
A Mother's Day Flower 40

Bible, the (God's Word)
Courtroom Drama 120

Brokenness
All Things New. 243

Busyness
Huge and Scary. 124

Change
All Things New. 243
At the Table of the King 27
One Way to America, Please 193
Something Changed 85
Uprooted. 128

Comfort
A Divine Embrace. 224

Compassion
Backpacker in the Rain 36
Beautiful Butterfly. 59
Lost and Found. 105
The Innkeeper. 66
The Least, the Lost, and the Lonely .135

Coping
The Little Mother 233

Courage
A Song in the Dark 147

Creation
Concert of Praise. 15
Fireflies 220
Star Struck 56

Disappointment
It's Not Fair 154

Dishonesty
Courtroom Drama 120

Divorce
All Things New. 243
I Surrender 108

Doubts
A Doubter's Prayer 198

Evangelism
Beautiful Butterfly. 59
Class Reunion 174
Crowds, Fish Oil, and Ego 161
The Power of Love 139

Faith
A Solid Foundation? 165
High Anxiety 12
Jailhouse Faith. 89
Nothing Is Impossible 7
The Blind Shall See. 23
The Sleep of the Innocent 97
Troubled Waters 177

Family
All Things New. 243
Raising Ashley. 43

Fatherhood
My Father's Taillights 143
The Sleep of the Innocent 97
Troubled Waters 177
Underwater Rescue 131

Fear
It Takes a Stable. 169
My Father's Taillights 143
Standing Guard. 188

Forgiveness
Dismissed!. 100
Freed to Forgive 78

Friendship
A Friend Few Can Claim. 237
Blunder Down Under 216
Class Reunion 174
Miss(ed) Hospitality 228
No Agenda 93
Nothing Is Impossible 7
The Unexpected Gift. 112

Future, plans for
Crowds, Fish Oil, and Ego 161

Giving
Free to Receive 180
The Least, the Lost, and the Lonely .135
The Unexpected Gift. 112

God
Faithfulness of
Free to Receive 180
It Takes a Stable. 169
The Worry Stone. 52
Troubled Waters 177

Family of
Two Daughters—One Father 18

Help from
Huge and Scary. 124
The Little Mother 233

Peace of
Turkey and Trouble 240
Uprooted. 128

Plans/Will of
Uncharted Territory. 116

Power of
Nothing Is Impossible 7

Presence of
Fireflies 220
I Surrender 108
The Writing on the Wall 202

Protection of
Sleepless .212
Standing Guard. 188

Provision of
A Boy for Brutus 31
Chance Meeting 150
Free to Receive 180
The Innkeeper. 66
Troubled Waters 177

Sovereignty of
Crowds, Fish Oil, and Ego 161

Time with
A Friend Few Can Claim. 237
A Solid Foundation? 165

Word of (See *Bible, the*)

Grace
Dismissed!. 100

Hardships
Raising Ashley. 43

Hospitality
Backpacker in the Rain 36
Miss(ed) Hospitality 228

Humility
All Things New. 243
Miss(ed) Hospitality 228
The Art of Toilet Scrubbing 157

Jesus
Birth of
At the Table of the King 27

Name of
"What's Your Friend's Name?" 81

Perfection of
Practice Doesn't Make Perfect 74

Kindness
Backpacker in the Rain 36
Lost and Found. 105

Loneliness
At the Table of the King 27

Love
for others
A Divine Embrace. 224
A Special Girl 206

of God
Beautiful Butterfly. 59
The Unexpected Gift. 112
Something Changed 85
Transformed by Love. 184

of Jesus
No Agenda 93
The Power of Love 139

Mentoring
More Than Words Can Say 209

Mercy
Backpacker in the Rain 36

Motherhood
A Mother's Day Flower 40
A Song in the Dark 147
A Special Girl 206
I Surrender 108
The Little Mother 233
The Worry Stone. 52
Transformed by Love. 184
Two Daughters—One Father 18
Whom Do You Trust? 48

Pain
The Path to Restoration 62

Parent, death of
A Divine Embrace. 224
Nothing Is Impossible 7
The Writing on the Wall 202
Uncharted Territory. 116

Patience
One Way to America, Please 193

Perfection
Practice Doesn't Make Perfect 74

Perseverance
The Blind Shall See. 23

Prayer
A Doubter's Prayer 198

A Friend Few Can Claim. 237
A Special Girl 206
Raising Ashley. 43
Underwater Rescue 131

Pride
Underwater Rescue 131

Rebellion
A Rebellious Sheep 70

Reconciliation
The Path to Restoration 62

Sin
A Rebellious Sheep 70

Single Parenting
All Things New. 243
I Surrender 108

Thankfulness
At the Table of the King 27
Turkey and Trouble 240

Trust in God
A Doubter's Prayer 198
A Song in the Dark 147
My Father's Taillights 143
One Way to America, Please 193
Sleepless .212
Whom Do You Trust? 48

Work
The Art of Toilet Scrubbing 157
Huge and Scary. 124

Worry
Sleepless .212
The Sleep of the Innocent 97
The Worry Stone. 52

Worship
Fireflies .220
Star Struck 56

Worth
Blunder Down Under 216

SCRIPTURE INDEX

Exodus 33:14
Fireflies. 220

Deuteronomy 31:8
The Writing on the Wall 202

Deuteronomy 33:27
The Writing on the Wall 202

Joshua 24:15
I Surrender. 108

2 Kings 6:15–17
Standing Guard 188

Psalm 19:1–4
Star Struck 56

Psalm 23:5–6
A Rebellious Sheep. 70

Psalm 25:4–5
Uncharted Territory 116

Psalm 27:5
Whom Do You Trust?. 48

Psalm 27:14
One Way to America, Please. 193

Psalm 29:11
Turkey and Trouble 240

Psalm 36:5–9
Transformed by Love 284

Psalm 100:1–3
Concert of Praise 15

Psalm 103:12
Dismissed! 100

Psalm 116:1–2
A Doubter's Prayer 198

Psalm 121
Sleepless 212

Psalm 139:16–18
Crowds, Fish Oil, and Ego 161

Proverbs 8:17
Jailhouse Faith 89

Proverbs 27:17
The Path to Restoration 62

Isaiah 26:3–4
High Anxiety 12

Isaiah 30:18
One Way to America, Please. 193

Isaiah 55:3
A Friend Few Can Claim 237

Isaiah 58:7–8
The Innkeeper 66

Jeremiah 17:7
It Takes a Stable 169

Jeremiah 18:1–6
All Things New 243

Jeremiah 29:11
It's Not Fair 154

Lamentations 3:23
Free to Receive 180

Ezekiel 36:26
The Power of Love 139

Zechariah 4:6
Huge and Scary 124

Matthew 5:46
More Than Words Can Say 209

Matthew 6:25–27
The Worry Stone 52

Matthew 6:30
A Mother's Day Flower. 40

Matthew 6:31–34
The Worry Stone 52

Matthew 6:34
The Sleep of the Innocent 97

Matthew 18:3
Nothing Is Impossible 7

Matthew 22:37–40
No Agenda. 93

Matthew 25:35
Backpacker in the Rain. 36

Matthew 25:40
The Least, the Lost,
and the Lonely 135

Matthew 28:20
Troubled Waters. 177

Mark 9:14–24
A Doubter's Prayer 198

Mark 11:25
Freed to Forgive 78

Luke 1:37
Nothing Is Impossible 7

Luke 4:18–19
The Blind Shall See 23

Luke 12:15
Blunder Down Under 216

John 10:14–15
"What's Your Friend's Name?" 81

John 10:27
My Father's Taillights 143

Romans 8:15
A Song in the Dark 147

2 Corinthians 1:3–4
A Divine Embrace 224

2 Corinthians 3:18
Something Changed. 85

2 Corinthians 5:21
Practice Doesn't Make Perfect. 74

2 Corinthians 10:17
Underwater Rescue. 131

Galatians 4:6–7
Two Daughters—One Father 18

Galatians 6:10
Lost and Found 105

Ephesians 1:3–14
Two Daughters—One Father 18

Ephesians 2:10
Lost and Found 105

Ephesians 3:20
Chance Meeting. 150

Ephesians 4:15
Practice Doesn't Make Perfect. 74

Ephesians 4:32
Beautiful Butterfly 59

Philippians 3:7–8
At the Table of the King 27

Philippians 4:6–7
The Sleep of the Innocent 97

Philippians 4:13
The Little Mother 233

Philippians 4:19
A Boy for Brutus 31
Chance Meeting. 150

Colossians 1:9–12
A Special Girl. 206

Colossians 3:13
Freed to Forgive 78

Colossians 3:23
The Art of Toilet Scrubbing 157

1 Thessalonians 5:17
Raising Ashley 43

2 Thessalonians 2:13–14
Class Reunion 174

2 Timothy 2:4
Uprooted 128

Hebrews 4:12
Courtroom Drama. 120

James 1:5–7
My Father's Taillights 143

James 5:20
More Than Words Can Say 209

1 Peter 4:8–10
Miss(ed) Hospitality. 228

1 John 4:7–8
The Unexpected Gift 112

Jude 20–21
A Solid Foundation?. 165